AT HIS DUSTY FEET

JUDITH HEANEY

At His Dusty Feet

Copyright © 2021 by
Judith Heaney

FIRST EDITION

www.judithheaney.com

Forward

It started with Ash Wednesday and a desire to do something during the 46 days of Lent. To do something that would draw me closer to Jesus and inspire a renewed intimacy with Him. For me, there is something wild and awe-inspiring about the extravagant love Jesus encompassed on His journey to Jerusalem, but also something breathtaking in the extravagant love some of His followers poured out on Him, in one case quite literally: the woman who washed His feet with an expensive perfume poured out from an alabaster jar.

Then, six days before the Passover, Jesus came to Bethany, where Lazarus lived, whom he had raised from the dead. So they prepared a dinner for Jesus there. Martha was serving, and Lazarus was among those present at the table with him. Then Mary took three quarters of a pound of expensive aromatic oil from pure nard and anointed the feet of Jesus. She then wiped his feet dry with her hair. (Now the house was filled with the fragrance of the perfumed oil.) But Judas Iscariot, one of his disciples (the one who was going to betray him) said, "Why wasn't this oil sold for three hundred silver coins and the money given to the poor?" (Now Judas said this not because he was concerned about the poor, but because he was a thief. As keeper of the money box, he used to steal what was put into it.) So Jesus said, "Leave her alone. She has kept it for the day of my burial. For you will always have the poor with you, but you will not always have me." John 12:1-8

When my connection to Jesus seems cursory and rote, my mind revisits this moment between Mary and Jesus. Mary always made Jesus the center of her attention when given the choice between Him and anything else. And this moment was no different but for how incredibly extravagant it was. So, when my own choice between Jesus and anything else becomes less than this, I long to restore that intimacy, that extravagance. I long for an expression of extravagant love in my life that will fill my life with the fragrance of nard poured out on Jesus' feet by me.

That's why I decided to walk with Jesus during His time in Jerusalem. I wanted to see Him through a raw and real love lived out in the moments on those dusty roads with His disciples. I wanted to choose Him over anything else, over *everything else*, and I wanted to know Him better than anyone or anything else. This devotional is the result of the choice to linger with Jesus like Mary, sitting close by Him, watching Him, listening to Him and simply *being* with Him. And even though it was a Lenten journey for me at the time, I came to realize that a 46-day journey with Jesus can be as useful during the summer or the fall or the winter as during Lent.

A journey with the Savior can be the cup of cold water your thirsty soul needs to cultivate an oasis of intimacy between you and Jesus at whatever time you need it. I hope this devotional and these words are that cup of cold water for you as you choose to linger with Jesus in Jerusalem.

> *Trust in the Lord, and do what is right.*
> *Settle in the land and maintain your integrity.*
> *Then you will take delight in the Lord,*
> *and he will answer your prayers.*
> **Psalm 37:3-4**

Table of Contents

Day 40: In the Eyes of Jesus

Now when they approached Jerusalem and came to Bethpage, at the Mount of Olives, Jesus sent two disciples, telling them, "Go to the village ahead of you. Right away you will find a donkey tied there, and a colt with her. Untie them and bring them to me. If anyone says anything to you, you are to say, 'The Lord needs them,' and he will send them at once." This took place to fulfill what was spoken by the prophet:

> **"Tell the people of Zion,**
> **'Look, your king is coming to you,**
> **unassuming and seated on a donkey,**
> **and on a colt, the foal of a donkey.'"**

So the disciples went and did as Jesus had instructed them. They brought the donkey and the colt and placed their cloaks on them, and he sat on them. A very large crowd spread their cloaks on the road. Others cut branches from the trees and spread them on the road. The crowds that went ahead of him and those following kept shouting, "Hosanna to the Son of David! **Blessed is the one who comes in the name of the Lord!** *Hosanna in the highest!" As he entered Jerusalem the whole city was thrown into an uproar, saying, "Who is this?" And the crowds were saying, "This is the prophet Jesus, from Nazareth in Galilee."* **Matthew 21:1-11**

Who is this?

"Behold, your king is coming to you, humble, and mounted on a donkey, on a colt, the foal of a beast of burden."

Yes, but who is He?

This is the prophet Jesus, from Nazareth of Galilee.

"Can anything good come out of Nazareth?" Nathanael asked when Philip invited him to come and meet the one Moses and the prophets wrote about. Nathanael was skeptical. His response was not surprising given what many believe about Nazareth: Nazareth was but a small remote village that does not play a major role in either the political or religious history of the Jews. To believe the Messiah could hail from such a place seems absurd.

This morning, however, they seem to believe He can come from such small beginnings and they even celebrate His arrival here in Jerusalem. This morning, I am standing with the crowd on the road into Jerusalem, watching and wondering. There is a lot of noise, voices are raised in song and celebration, but also in questioning. Jesus rides on a donkey. He quotes scripture, indicating it is being fulfilled right now, in this very moment. I wonder, does the crowd understand what He's telling them?

Around Him is chaos and it seems maybe they don't fully understand His declaration.

We don't know it, watching Him enter Jerusalem, but everything is about to change. Right now, we shout and celebrate. This moment requires nothing more of us than joy. It is easy to join in and so I do.

Watching Him, following Him, my stomach flutters with a sense of anticipation. The energy around Him is electric; something big is about to happen. I can feel it. I can see it in His eyes. Though the crowd is singing and shouting and stirred up in jubilee, His eyes tell a different story. Does anyone else notice? Is anyone else seeing this King and the story His eyes tell?

He knows something the rest of us don't and it's there, in His eyes. There is a sadness there. Or maybe it is resignation? While the people swirl around me in celebration, I stop shouting and stare at Him, trying to take Him in, trying to discern what I see. I want to see Him for who He is.

As I watch Him, as I study His face taking in the faces of the crowd that surrounds Him, I recognize what I see in His eyes is compassion. It is love. An extravagant, unconditional love.

This extravagant love flows out from Him and it is palpable. It wraps around me like an embrace. It comforts me, though I didn't realize I needed comforting. It draws me to Him and it is why I follow Him even though I am jostled and crushed by the throng of jumping, dancing, exuberant people.

When He looks at me, I start. For a moment, I feel compelled to look away. Shame creeps into my consciousness and I remember so many of the bad choices I've made. I am not worthy of this king, humble though He appears. But I don't look away. Something in His eyes holds mine. They say it's okay; it's all going to be okay.

His eyes speak words only my heart can hear. They convey His extravagant, unconditional, passionate love for me.

Even so, I am afraid. I am afraid because I know He sees me, *all* of me. I am afraid because His love is overwhelming and yet

3

intimate. I am afraid because I know that as this king, this Jesus, enters Jerusalem, the rules are going to change.

It's all right there, in His eyes. His eyes betray His determination as well as His love. He has come for a reason. He is *here* for a reason.

There is purpose in His eyes, in His riding on a donkey, in His very being, in His every breath. Everything He has done up to this point has led Him here. It has led all of us here.

And so we enter Jerusalem. Together. As He enters the city my sense of anticipation ignites a desire in me to draw near to Him. To stay close to Him. To follow Him. To love Him, with as extravagant a love as I am able. Even if I am afraid of what that love will require, which I am beginning to realize as I watch Him move slowly through the crowded street is nothing less than all of me.

Prayer

Dear Heavenly Father, thank You for your unconditional and sacrificial love that brought Jesus here. Despite the lies of the enemy that tell me that I am unworthy, Your invitation to walk with Jesus, and to join Him here in Jerusalem reminds me how much You love me. It also reminds me that I will not love You with anything less than all of me. You are a refuge and Your throne of grace is open to me to pour out my heart: my cares, my dreams, my fears, and, by doing so, to find peace in Your presence. Though I have at times rejected or denied your Son by my choices, I seek Him now. I seek to know Him and You and walk with You in intimate friendship. I pray these things in Jesus' name. Amen.

Additional Scripture for Reflection

Esther 4:10-17

Psalm 118:22-26

Psalm 62:5-8

Day 39: In the Company of Judas Iscariot

Then, six days before the Passover, Jesus came to Bethany, where Lazarus lived, whom he had raised from the dead. So they prepared a dinner for Jesus there. Martha was serving, and Lazarus was among those present at the table with him. Then Mary took three quarters of a pound of expensive aromatic oil from pure nard and anointed the feet of Jesus. She then wiped his feet dry with her hair. (Now the house was filled with the fragrance of the perfumed oil.) But Judas Iscariot, one of his disciples (the one who was going to betray him) said, "Why wasn't this oil sold for three hundred silver coins and the money given to the poor?" (Now Judas said this not because he was concerned about the poor, but because he was a thief. As keeper of the money box, he used to steal what was put into it.) So Jesus said, "Leave her alone. She has kept it for the day of my burial. For you will always have the poor with you, but you will not always have me." **John 12:1-8**

Today, on the journey to Jerusalem, we stop in Bethany, the place where Lazarus lives. The Lazarus who lives because Jesus raised him from the dead. And so, I recline with Jesus and Lazarus at the table. But my focus is not on Jesus as we sit around this table. It is on Judas Iscariot and Lazarus and the incredible difference in their responses to Jesus.

Judas exudes what feels like a sense of duty and obligation combined with unmet expectations. Jesus is neither who Judas wants Him to be nor who Judas expected and hoped He would be. Rather than a warrior king sent to defeat Israel's enemies once and for all, Jesus is a rebel of redemption and a humble servant who takes on the religious elite rather than the Roman rulers. Unlike Judas, Lazarus radiates absolute, resolute joy; it's in his smile, in the way his eyes light up as he speaks to and listens to Jesus, and in the relaxed, reclining position he has taken at the table near his dear friend and redeemer.

I cannot help but compare Lazarus' joy-filled demeanor with Judas' more stoic and business-like manner. Where Lazarus is comfortable and relaxed, Judas is tense and sharp, both in tone and posture. In the midst of this celebratory evening among friends, Judas' response to Mary's actions feels entirely out of place, and Jesus is quick to address it. He defends Mary's extravagance, and in doing so, he convicts Judas for his greed and for his misplaced focus.

Does Judas feel Jesus' rebuke? It's difficult to say. Knowing that Judas, like the other 11 disciples, has been with Jesus throughout His three years of ministry and witnessed miracles and listened to Jesus' words, how is it Judas remains reserved and reticent in the presence of this king? Who exactly is this man who travels with Jesus? I know where some of the other disciples come from and how Jesus called them to follow Him. But Judas? I don't know much about him.

And so today I contemplate him. I wonder, was he as willing and eager to follow Jesus as Simon and Andrew, who dropped everything the moment Jesus invited them to follow Him? Did Judas have reservations even then, or was he so excited by the idea

Jesus might possibly be the Messiah for whom he'd been waiting that he left all he knew without hesitation? I can't help but believe he must have been excited at least initially. So when did that change for Judas? When did the reservations set in and when did he decide to steal from Jesus, or, even worse, to withdraw from Jesus?

I watch Judas. I watch the indifference he seems to have toward Jesus. I watch him bristle at the extravagance Mary demonstrates. And I cannot help but marvel at his mock indignation, claiming the perfume could have been sold to help the poor. How can he be in the presence of Jesus, not just around this table, but for three years now, and not be changed? How is it possible for him to be in the presence of Jesus and yet not embrace who Jesus is? Not embrace such powerful, unconditional love. Not embrace hope. Not embrace what Jesus is about and who Jesus is.

And yet even as I watch Judas with his indignation and seemingly duplicitous nature and even as I feel my own overwhelming love flowing from my heart for this Jesus who loves me with all my flaws, I wonder.

How many times have I looked more to my gain than to my Savior? How many times have I, like Judas, missed the opportunity to see before me the plans, the messy truth lurking in my own messed up heart? How many times have I sat in the presence of Jesus with ambivalence, distracted by my own agenda, my own needs, my own desires? How many times?

I can't count.

And so, today, I am thankful as I sit around this table where Martha serves and Mary worships and Lazarus adores for an opportunity to examine my own heart and my own motivations.

Today, I am willing to look at the deep, dark places and ask Jesus to shine His light there. To seek forgiveness for the times I have put my desires for gain above my need for Jesus. To seek forgiveness for chasing personal gain instead of helping others. To seek forgiveness for my Judas moments.

Prayer

Dear Jesus, sometimes I forget I have moments that look more like Judas than Mary or Lazarus. Thank you for the grace you pour out when I come to you and confess my sins and my selfishness. Jesus, search my heart and shine your light into the dark places, and help me to release my grip on those things that only bring me pain or are good enough rather than your best and your joy and abundant love. It is in your forgiveness and grace I find the abundant life you so freely give.

Additional Scripture for Reflection

John 8:4-11

Matthew 7:2-4

Psalm 139:23-24

Day 38: The Dead Come to Life

The next day the large crowd that had come to the feast heard that Jesus was coming to Jerusalem. So they took branches of palm trees and went out to meet him. They began to shout, **"Hosanna! Blessed is the one who comes in the name of the Lord!** *Blessed is the king of Israel!"* *Jesus found a young donkey and sat on it, just as it is written,* **"Do not be afraid, people of Zion; look, your king is coming, seated on a donkey's colt!"** *(His disciples did not understand these things when they first happened, but when Jesus was glorified, then they remembered that these things were written about him and that these things had happened to him.)*

So the crowd who had been with him when he called Lazarus out of the tomb and raised him from the dead were continuing to testify about it. Because they had heard that Jesus had performed this miraculous sign, the crowd went out to meet him. Thus the Pharisees said to one another, "You see that you can do nothing. Look, the world has run off after him!" **John 12:12-19**

Can you imagine what it was like to be Lazarus?

He isn't one of the 12 Apostles, but he is a dear friend of Jesus. And he is here to celebrate Jesus coming to Jerusalem. But he is as much a celebrity as Jesus. Maybe more so. Many in the crowd are talking about when Lazarus stepped out of the tomb alive and well. That's one of the things that has brought so many people to come and see Jesus today.

Who wouldn't want to see, hear, touch, and meet the person who brought a man back from the dead? This man who called Lazarus out of the tomb four days after he'd been lain inside and the tomb sealed.

But what about Lazarus? What is he thinking? I can't help but wonder as I watch him celebrating his friend's arrival. As I watch the smile spreading across his face and radiating the incredible joy and gratitude that clearly fills him as he watches his friend. *His savior.*

Having experienced death and resurrection, does he see things differently? Does he see and understand things about Jesus we don't yet see or know or understand?

Standing here in the midst of the crowd I yearn to make my way over to Lazarus' side and pull him away from the crowd. Apart from the crowds and the chaos, I long to bend his ear and to ask him what it was like to die. Did he go to heaven? Did he see God? Did he *talk* with God? Did he witness the mourning of his friends and his sisters that came before the joy that dawned at the sound of Jesus' voice calling him out of the grave?

I want Lazarus to tell me everything he's thinking, everything he knows as we stand together and watch the crowd swell around Jesus.

I want him to share what he knows of God and Jesus and heaven. I want to know what it's like to be close to Jesus. I want to know what it's like to be so intimately loved by Jesus He wept for you, He restored you, He resurrected you.

But those are not Lazarus' secrets alone, are they? Jesus loves me. He has wept for me, He has collected my tears (Psalm 56:8), He has restored me, and He has redeemed me, resurrected me from who I was into who He created me to be in and with Him.

Jesus is here in Jerusalem for me. When He looks at me, I can sense His love for me. It is as strong a love as the one He shares with Lazarus. It is the same deep love with which he spoke Lazarus' name, calling Lazarus back from death and from the grave.

Like Lazarus, this man I am watching and whom I stand beside, this Jesus will bring me back to life. In fact, He has countless times. No, not by calling me from the grave, but by calling me out of the pit of despair, calling me out of temptation and sin, calling me out of myself, toward Him, where He breathes new life into me.

Just like He did with Lazarus, He calls me by my name. He sees me. He loves me.

Even as I stand here with Lazarus, I hear the song I sing every night at bedtime to my girls, *Jesus Loves Me*, except that ever since they were babies I have sung it as, *Jesus Loves You*, reminding my girls - and myself - we are loved by the Creator. When you sing these words enough, when you hear these words enough - *Jesus loves you* - they take on a bigger, deeper meaning.

I am weak. He loves me anyway.

I am afraid. He loves me anyway.

I am needy. He loves me anyway. (In fact, He loves this about me because He knows I need Him.)

I am messed up and I mess up. He loves me anyway.

I get lost and wander away. He loves me anyway.

I get angry. He loves me anyway.

I get prideful and self-sufficient. He loves me anyway.

He loves me because He created me and called me to Himself and He sees who I am when I am rooted in Him. He is Life, and He wants to share that Life -- *His life* -- with me.

This journey to Jerusalem is filled with truths like these, and even though I wasn't quite convinced I wanted to take this trip with Him, Jesus is okay with that and calls me forth anyway. He is okay with my faltering steps and my doubts because He sees the desires of my heart.

The desire that longs for Him and pursues Him and leaves the darkness behind for Him. The desire to draw near to Him in spite of my fear. The desire to know the celebration that comes when I choose to follow Him.

The desire to come to Life.

Prayer

Dear Jesus, thank you that you know me and that you see me, and that you always hear me. How amazing that you sought me even before I knew you or knew I needed you. Thank you for restoring me to wholeness. I know that you love me even when I mess up and turn away or miss your presence. Thank you, Jesus, for your love that pursues me and gives me Life.

Additional Scripture for Reflection

John 11:38-44

1 John 4:9-12

2 Corinthians 5:15-21

Day 37: Fig Trees, Fruit, and Faith

*Then Jesus entered the temple area and drove out all those who were selling and buying in the temple courts, and turned over the tables of the money changers and the chairs of those selling doves. And he said to them, "It is written, **'My house will be called a house of prayer,'** but you are turning it into **a den of robbers!"***

*The bind and the lame came to him in the temple courts, and he healed them. But when the chief priests and the experts in the law saw the wonderful things he did and heard the children crying out in the temple courts, "Hosanna to the Son of David," they became indignant and said to him, "Do you hear what they are saying?" Jesus said to them, "Yes. Have you never read, **'Out of the mouths of children and nursing infants you have prepared praise for yourself**?" And leaving them, he went out of the city to Bethany and spent the night there.*

Now early in the morning, as he returned to the city, he was hungry. After noticing a fig tree by the road he went to it, but found nothing on it except leaves. He said to it, "Never again will there be fruit from you!" And the fig tree withered at once. When the disciples saw it they were amazed, saying, "How did the fig tree wither so quickly?"

Jesus answered them, "I tell you the truth, if you have faith and do not doubt, not only will you do what was done to the fig tree, but even if you say to this mountain, ' Be lifted up and thrown into the sea,' it will happen. **Matthew 21:12-21**

It is early and the crowds of yesterday have not yet returned. In the quiet, I watch with the disciples as Jesus approaches a leafy fig tree a short distance away. He is hungry and He is hoping to enjoy some of its fruit. But it has no fruit to offer.

In what seems like an uncharacteristic response, Jesus curses the lonely tree. His strong words seem unwarranted and they confuse me. But do I dare question this moment? And yet how can I not? Because when we pass by the same tree the next morning, it has withered and died.

It seems incongruous, this response from Jesus to a fig tree. It isn't even the time for it to bear fruit. Or is it?

The tree is full of lush, green leaves. Yes, it is out of season, but there are the leaves. This alone indicates that there may be fruit. But Jesus is not as interested in the fig tree and its fruit, or lack of it, as He is in the fruit, or lack of it, of His followers.

Jesus' response to the fig tree is not so incongruous after all. He sees a teaching moment and He takes it. He has, after all, come to Jerusalem to die and to redeem. The shouts of celebration, the leafy green response of the crowds, will soon turn to demands for His death. Jerusalem will wither. Hope will die.

Religion will conquer faith.

In recent days, as Jesus prepares for the Passover meal here, His run-ins with the Pharisees and religious leaders are increasing. There is talk of their true feelings about Jesus and the following He has created; they have contradicted, undermined, and argued with Him since He began His public ministry, but their desire to destroy His ministry - to destroy Him - has escalated exponentially.

Jesus knows the stakes are high. He knows each of His actions is stirring the hearts of the religious leaders to deep hatred. Because of this, He knows His disciples need to understand what is coming. In His true teaching ways, Jesus uses a lonely fig tree that is blooming out of season to make His point: the leafy green appearance of many does not necessarily translate into the fruit of faith or knowing Jesus.

Point taken.

Looking upon the now-withered fig tree, I take a moment to examine myself, to look into my heart, and consider my motivations. Am I bearing fruit? Or am I simply outwardly playing a good part, seeming to bear fruit from a distance, but withering in my faith upon closer examination? Am I a Pharisee? Am I more religious than faith-filled?

If Jesus approached me, drew near to me, expecting fruit, what would He find?

Prayer

Dear Jesus, thank you for your promises and for your teaching moments, which have sometimes been more numerous in my life than I care to acknowledge. But you are always willing to prune away the dead parts so that I might bear fruit and not wither. Thank you that I am redeemed and that you are intimately interested in me and seeing me thrive daily in the abundant life you alone provide.

Additional Scripture for Reflection

John 15:1-8

Galatians 5:22-26

1 Samuel 16:7

A Day of Reading and Reflection

Additional Scripture for Reflection

Genesis 9:8-17

God said to Noah and his sons, "Look. I now confirm my covenant with you and your descendants after you and with every living creature that is with you, including the bird, the domestic animals, and every living creature of the earth with you, all those that came out of the ark with you—every living creature of the earth. I confirm my covenant with you: Never again will all living things be wiped out by the waters of a flood; never again will a flood destroy the earth."

And God said, "This is the guarantee of the covenant I am making with you and every living creature with you, a covenant for all subsequent generations: I will place my rainbow in the clouds, and it will become a guarantee of the covenant between me and the earth."

So God said to Noah, "This is the guarantee of the covenant that I am confirming between me and all living things that are on the earth."

Psalm 25:1-10

O LORD, I come before you in prayer.
My God, I trust in you.
Please do not let me be humiliated;
do not let my enemies triumphantly rejoice over me.
Certainly none who rely on you will be humiliated.

19

*Those who deal in treachery will be thwarted and
    humiliated.*
Make me understand your ways, O LORD.
Teach me your paths.
Guide me into your truth and teach me.
For you are the God who delivers me;
on you I rely all day long.
*Remember your compassionate and faithful deeds,
    O LORD,*
for you have always acted in this manner.
*Do not hold against me the sins of my youth or my
    rebellious acts.*
*Because you are faithful to me, extend to me your
    favor, O LORD.*
The LORD is both kind and fair;
that is why he teaches sinners the right way to live.
May he show the humble what is right.
May he teach the humble his way.
The LORD always proves faithful and reliable
to those who follow the demands of his covenant.

1 Peter 3:18-2

*Because Christ also suffered once for sins the just
for the unjust, to bring you to God, by being put to death
in the flesh but by being made alive in the spirit.*

*In it he went and preached to the spirits in prison,
after they were disobedient long ago when God patiently
waited in the days of Noah as an ark was being
constructed. In the ark a few, that is eight souls, were
delivered through water. And this prefigured baptism,*

which now saves you—not the washing off of physical dirt but the pledge of a good conscience to God—through the resurrection of Jesus Christ, who went into heaven and is at the right hand of God with angels and authorities and powers subject to him.

Mark 1:9-15

Now in those days Jesus came from Nazareth in Galilee and was baptized by John in the Jordan River. And just as Jesus was coming up out of the water, he saw the heavens splitting apart and the Spirit descending on him like a dove. And a voice came from heaven: "You are my one dear Son; in you I take great delight." The Spirit immediately drove him into the wilderness. He was in the wilderness 40 days, enduring temptations from Satan. He was with wild animals, and angels were ministering to his needs.

Now after John was imprisoned, Jesus went into Galilee and proclaimed the gospel of God. He said, "The time is fulfilled and the kingdom of God is near. Repent and believe the gospel!"

Day 36: The Fruit of Faith

Now the next day, as they went out from Bethany, he was hungry. After noticing in the distance a fig tree with leaves, he went to see if he could find any fruit on it. When he came to it he found nothing but leaves, for it was not the season for figs. He said to it, "May no one ever eat fruit from you again." And his disciples heard it.

*Then they came to Jerusalem. Jesus entered the temple area and began to drive out those who were selling and buying in the temple courts. He turned over the tables of the money changers and the chairs of those selling doves, and he would not permit anyone to carry merchandise through the temple courts. Then he began to teach them and said, "Is it not written: '**My house will be called a house of prayer for all nations**'? But you have turned it into **a den of robbers**!" The chief priests and the experts in the law heard it and they considered how they could assassinate him, for they feared him, because the whole crowd was amazed by his teaching. When evening came, Jesus and his disciples went out of the city.*

In the morning as they passed by, they saw the fig tree withered from the roots. Peter remembered and said to him, "Rabbi, look! The fig tree you cursed has withered." Jesus said to them, "Have faith in God. I tell you the truth, if someone says to this mountain, 'Be lifted up and thrown into the sea,' and does not doubt in his heart but believes that what he says will happen, it will be done for him. For this reason I tell you, whatever you pray and ask for, believe that you have received it, and it will be yours. Whenever you stand praying, if you have anything against anyone, forgive him, so that your Father in heaven will also forgive you your sins." **Mark 11:12-26**

I follow Jesus into the temple expecting a sacred experience with Him, expecting to listen to Him teach, and to gain wisdom I can store in my heart and rely on in the living out of my story in this world. After all, we are gathered here in a holy space with Jesus. If anything embodies the God part of this man who is wholly man and wholly God, it's the temple where God's people come to pray and to worship, right?

None of what happens next meets my expectations. Instead of a serene scene of sacred reverence, it is a bustling place of loud and overwhelming chaos. All around the outer vestibule lambs, oxen, and sheep are tied or penned up, their constant bleating and lowing accost me immediately along with the cooing and flapping of pigeons, all of them for sale. And then there is the smell; it is like being in a stable that needs to be cleaned. Over the din of the animals come human voices shouting as innumerable sellers hawk their wares and still others protest and argue over the inflated prices being charged to buy animals for sacrifice and to exchange money for the temple tax. I am tempted to turn and leave. How can anyone focus on God in the midst of all of this commotion?

As I try to acclimate to the scene and surroundings, I watch Jesus take in the scene. It takes Him less than a minute to amplify the already deafening cacophony. If not for the fact that He is *God with us*, His rage would stir a deep fear within me. This is not a side of Jesus with which I am familiar. Nor am I comfortable with it. He is angry. Beyond angry, really. He shouts at people and flips over tables in pure rage. He rants about the treatment of His Father's house. His otherwise gentle eyes blaze with a ferocity and passion that cause me to back away from Him.

This is the zeal for His Father's house he has alluded to, but until now I did not fully understand. Now, standing in the middle of this mayhem, I understand his deep passion. His passion is clearly of the One through whom all things were made. This is His Father's house, but it is also *His* house. The place where God's people are meant to come and worship the God who loves them and to seek His mercy, His grace, His forgiveness, and His presence. But God is not the focus here. These sellers and money changers have made a mockery of the sacred traditions; their focus is on profit and business as they take advantage of those who have traveled great distances to be here.

As Jesus continues making His way through the crowd, there is at first greater chaos in His wake as animals are herded out of the temple and table wares and coins are scattered across the stones beneath our feet. Until at last, slowly, a calm settles around me, the crowd's initial shock transitioning into awe for some, understanding for others, and resentment for still others. The indignation and resentment of the chief priests and scribes is obvious on their faces, especially when Jesus refers to His Father's House as a den of robbers.

His truth pierces their appearance of holiness. They know that as much as Jesus does. There is a tension between them—Jesus and these religious leaders—as they square off in this sacred space. Where earlier I was a bit fearful *of* Jesus because of His outrage, now I am fearful *for* Him because of it. The eyes of the rulers belie their desire to discredit Him, to undermine Him, and to destroy Him. But they are reluctant to act on their desires because they, like me, can see the crowd's astonishment at Jesus and His teaching. They fear the crowds too much to challenge Jesus in this moment, but I can tell from their expressions, they will not wait much longer to act. Their hatred is as strong as it is obvious.

Even so, I pity these rulers because they just don't get it. They do not want to change their ways because they are comfortable with what they've created and what their lives look like. They do just enough to appear like good people, but their hearts reveal a different story and Jesus knows it. And by their reactions to Him, they seem to know it, too. But maybe it's because I see myself in them that I see this in them. Not the me that has followed Jesus here today, but the me I was before I chose to follow Him.

It is easy to convince ourselves that we are good enough the way we are. For me, if I compare myself to others, I can easily become like the Pharisees and the religious leaders; I can elevate myself to seem better and to appear better than I am. In other words, I can bury my flaws, hide them away from myself and others. But when I come into the Light, into the presence of Jesus, those flaws burn brighter in spite of my attempts to hide them away. In the light of His holiness, Jesus calls me not only to face my shortcomings, but to acknowledge them, to repent and genuinely turn away from those things and turn toward Him.

But the Pharisees are not interested in this. They do not want any part of admitting they are not who they have portrayed themselves to be to the crowds. To do so is to give up the status they have orchestrated. To do so is to admit they are in need of mercy and forgiveness. The hardness in their eyes matches the hardness of their hearts, and still Jesus seeks them. Just like he seeks all of the lost. Just like he seeks me when I lose who I am and who He calls me to be in the lie of who I think I am when I measure myself against other imperfect people.

Because His zeal for His Father's house in this moment is matched only by His zeal for the lost. His zeal for the Pharisees. His zeal for you. And His zeal for me.

Prayer

Dear Jesus, thank you for your zeal in pursuing me and for caring about my heart more than how I look to myself or the world. Thank you for loving me and for calling me into Your light and Your presence. I acknowledge there are times when I think more highly of myself than I should because rather than looking at myself as I am reflected in Your light, I look at myself in comparison to other flawed, less-than-perfect people in this world. As I move forward from this place, I pray you would prompt me to surrender my heart always first to You as Your dwelling place, remembering Your desire for my heart to desire You.

Additional Scripture for Reflection

Psalm 139:1-12

Ephesians 3:14-21

Luke 6:43-45

Day 35: Crowding Out My Faith

Now after Jesus entered the temple courts, the chief priests and elders of the people came up to him as he was teaching and said, "By what authority are you doing these things, and who gave you this authority?" Jesus answered them, "I will also ask you one question. If you answer me then I will also tell you by what authority I do these things. Where did John's baptism come from? From heaven or from people?" They discussed this among themselves, saying, "If we say, 'From heaven,' he will say, 'Then why did you not believe him?' But if we say, 'From people,' we fear the crowd, for they all consider John to be a prophet." So they answered Jesus, "We don't know." Then he said to them, "Neither will I tell you by what authority I am doing these things.

"What do you think? A man had two sons. He went to the first and said, 'Son, go and work in the vineyard today.' The boy answered, 'I will not.' But later he had a change of heart and went. The father went to the other son and said the same thing. This boy answered, 'I will, sir,' but did not go. Which of the two did his father's will?" They said, "The first." Jesus said to them, "I tell you the truth, tax collectors and prostitutes will go ahead of you into the kingdom of God! For John came to you in the way of righteousness, and you did not believe him. But the tax collectors and prostitutes did believe. Although you saw this, you did not later change your minds and believe him. **Matthew 21:23-32**

Standing in the shadows inside the Temple, I shift uncomfortably from one foot to the other. Things are getting extremely intense. I don't know if the crowds sense it yet, but the leading priests, the elders, the religious leaders definitely do. Every interaction between Jesus and these leaders is a confrontation, a calling out by Jesus of the posturing and public hypocrisy these priests and Pharisees embody. The truth and conviction of Jesus' words strike hard and the resulting fear is palpable.

But it is not the truth they fear. Nor is it this man Jesus they fear, at least not in the way they should.

Yes, they fear His popularity. Yes, they fear His ability to lead the people, *their* people, away from them. Yes, they fear His influence on the crowds. But they do not fear Him, this man Jesus. This Son of God. This Word made flesh. He is the One with the power to convict and the power to redeem. But they are not afraid of Him.

Whom do they fear? They fear the crowds.

When pressed with Jesus' questions or presented with Jesus' parables revealing their love of religion and lack of genuine faith, their anger flares. In the face of His accusations their response is to ask, *how dare He say such things about them* instead of considering how they might do things differently. Like defendants at their trial, like witnesses under fire, they confer in whispered tones. They weigh their options. They consider the crowd's reaction to their response.

Even in this moment, standing close to them, watching their actions and reactions, I can see they are not concerned with answering the question; what they believe about John remains hidden by their words that deflect their heart's true desires.

28

As I witness their exchange with Jesus from the shadows, I watch them convict themselves by their words and their actions. Their efforts to undermine Jesus before the crowds once again reveals more about them and their sense of self and their perceived righteousness. They are not concerned with the truth or with the origin of John's authority to baptize. They are concerned with how they look, how they are perceived by others. They are concerned with how they appear to the crowd.

Watching them, I see myself in them and I sink deeper into the shadows to reflect on this revelation. This *truth*.

How many times have I worried more about what others think about me than what Jesus thinks of me? I worry what the crowd - the world - thinks about these words I write. I worry what the crowd - the world - thinks about me because I believe in and trust in Jesus. I worry what the crowd - the world - thinks about my impetuous Simon-Peter convictions and resulting actions or my belief that right and wrong is not relative.

Growing up and sometimes even now, faith and life are considered separate pursuits. The first is lived out in private and the second is lived out in the world at large, and ne'er the two shall meet. Declarations of faith and trust in Jesus, were often met with a polite smile, like a patronizing pat on the head. The implication imbued with the sentiment,

if that works for you, great, but I have my own truth.

And without pause, too often I choose the acceptance of others over my relationship with Jesus. I was afraid of the crowds, whether the crowd was my family, my friends or the world at large. I wanted their acceptance. I wanted their approval. I wanted to fit in, to belong, to blend in.

If I am not intentional, I fall back into this way of thinking and being. The world feels so immediate and their judgments so much more real. They are, in a sense, at least on this side of eternity. But where does that leave Jesus?

Where does that leave me?

Every day offers abundant life, but that looks different depending on the lens through which I view it. I can have joy that is not influenced by my circumstances but comes from my intimate connection with Jesus, or I can have happiness, a happiness that is fleeting because it is dependent upon my circumstances and how I'm feeling about my life. But I have learned feelings do not gage Truth and therefore often distort the difference between joy (contentment in Christ) and happiness.

I can accept Jesus' reproach, repent, and live redeemed or I can seek the crowd's approval.

I can live for today or I can live for eternity.

I can hide Jesus and horde Him, letting others fend for themselves, or I can leak Jesus into the world and the lives around me.

This journey through Jerusalem is demanding. It requires more of me than I anticipated or could have imagined. And I am thankful for the opportunity to witness all of these things, these things Jesus is doing and the events of His journey, because these things are becoming a part of my journey.

Prayer

Dear Jesus, it's one thing to say that I trust you and that I will follow you, but it's another thing entirely to do these things. The voice of the crowd is loud and its influence is sometimes too much for me to bear without caving in to the pressure to be like the world. But you call me to be in the world, not of it. Thank you for being my strength so I can follow you boldly and shine my light before others.

Additional Scripture for Reflection

Luke 14:25-34

Matthew 5:13-16

Romans 12:1-2

Day 34: Jesus: Rebel of Redemption

Jesus spoke to them again in parables, saying: "The kingdom of heaven can be compared to a king who gave a wedding banquet for his son. He sent his slaves to summon those who had been invited to the banquet, but they would not come. Again he sent other slaves, saying, 'Tell those who have been invited, "Look! The feast I have prepared for you is ready. My oxen and fattened cattle have been slaughtered, and everything is ready. Come to the wedding banquet."' But they were indifferent and went away, one to his farm, another to his business. The rest seized his slaves, insolently mistreated them, and killed them. The king was furious! He sent his soldiers, and they put those murderers to death and set their city on fire. Then he said to his slaves, 'The wedding is ready, but the ones who had been invited were not worthy. So go into the main streets and invite everyone you find to the wedding banquet.' And those slaves went out into the streets and gathered all they found, both bad and good, and the wedding hall was filled with guests. But when the king came in to see the wedding guests, he saw a man there who was not wearing wedding clothes. And he said to him, 'Friend, how did you get in here without wedding clothes?' But he had nothing to say. Then the king said to his attendants, 'Tie him up hand and foot and throw him into the outer darkness, where there will be weeping *gnashing of teeth!' For many are called, but few are chosen." **Matthew 22:1-14***

Another parable. Another story meant to make a point. Another timely message that falls on deaf ears. Except for mine.

Today I sit in the presence of Jesus rapt in His explosive passion and I am reminded of the times He has confronted me with the truth about who I am versus who I am created to be in Him; He has called me out on behaviors I've worked hard to rationalize or gloss over. In the light of His truth and His love, the reality of what I was doing became far more difficult to disguise as righteous.

Sitting here now, listening to His words, once again I am both awed and intimidated by the righteous anger that radiates from Him; it is unrelenting, and yet it is wrapped in His incredible and unconditional love. Do the Pharisees sense the depth of His love like I do?

If they do, neither their words nor their actions say so. Given this opportunity to know Jesus, to know this man that stands before them, they refuse to accept Him or His Truth. They refuse to know Him or love Him. They refuse to truly see Him. Or maybe they do, and that is why they despise Him. Even more, they don't even seem to acknowledge the opportunity He sets before them yet again, an opportunity for forgiveness, redemption, and change.

Of course if they don't see a need for these things, how will they see the opportunity set before them? Nor will they see the compassion - the love - that stirs Jesus to action today. The Pharisees are blind to their part in why Jesus has come to Jerusalem today. Instead of seeing someone who has come to help and to heal, they see a rebel who is trying to undermine them, along with the prestigious life they have so carefully curated. Rather than a savior, they see a rebel who is trying to ruin their lives by upending not only their status, but the status quo.

It can feel like that sometimes, though, can't it?

It feels that way right now as Jesus takes aim at the hearts of the Pharisees because above all else, He cares about their hearts. I believe He is concerned with the way the Pharisees are behaving and how they have corrupted what God intended for good for His people. But the events over the three years leading to this moment in Jerusalem show Jesus is more interested in peoples' hearts than in their actions *or* sins. His actions are motivated by His unconditional love, His grace, His willingness to forgive, and His willingness to give us abundant life.

Yes, He admonished the woman at the well (who had been with several different men), the woman caught in adultery (who was dragged before Him for condemnation), the rich young ruler (who was unwilling to give up his possessions), and the disciples (who sometimes just didn't "get it" despite how long they'd been with Him). But He loved all of them as much before He called them out as He did after (and His love for the rich young ruler never wavered even when the young man couldn't make a commitment to Jesus over his personal possessions). This is this same acceptance He offers the Pharisees in each encounter, including this one; He offers them grace, forgiveness, and love. Always love.

He offers us the same things, but it doesn't feel like that sometimes. I have uttered more times than I can count the words, *Why are you doing this to me?!* Sometimes it feels like Jesus is trying to ruin your life when He stands in front of you and calls you out and confronts you. And convicts you. When His words convict you, you have a choice. You can choose to change, like the woman at the well or the woman caught in adultery, or, like the Pharisees, you can choose self-righteous indignation and convince yourself it's Jesus who is wrong, not you.

Letting Jesus take away the sin in your life is beyond humbling and beyond painful. It is excruciating. It can feel like He is ruining your life. But really, He's redeeming it. He's refining it. He's *redefining* it, and you, in the process. He really is every bit the rebel the Pharisees feared. He is a rebel of redemption.

Prayer

Dear Jesus, thank you for being relentless in your pursuit of me and for loving me so much that you poured out your blood to cover my sins and to make me whiter than snow. Thank you, too, for your Truth that reminds me daily I am loved unconditionally and I can do nothing to earn or lose that amazing love. Thank you for opening my eyes to your Truth and for being the Rebel of Redemption who forgives and redeems and loves instead of condemning or shaming or rejecting. Make me a rebel, too.

Additional Scripture for Reflection

John 4:1-26

John 8:1-11

Proverbs 16:1-9

Day 33: The Contradiction of Faith

Then he began to speak to them in parables: "A man planted a vineyard. He put a fence around it, dug a pit for its winepress and built a watchtower. Then he leased it to tenant farmers and went on a journey. At harvest time he sent a slave to the tenants to collect from them his portion of the crop. But those tenants seized his slave, beat him, and sent him away empty-handed. So he sent another slave to them again. This one they struck on the head and treated outrageously. He sent another, and that one they killed. This happened to many others, some of whom were beaten, others killed. He had one left, his one dear son. Finally he sent him to them, saying, 'They will respect my son.' But those tenants said to one another, 'This is the heir. Come, let's kill him and the inheritance will be ours! So they seized him, killed him, and threw his body out of the vineyard. What then will the owner of the vineyard do? He will come and destroy those tenants and give the vineyard to others. Have you not read this scripture:

*"'**The stone the builders rejected has become the cornerstone.***

This is from the Lord, and it is marvelous in our eyes'?"

Now they wanted to arrest him (but they feared the crowd), because they realized that he told this parable *against them. So they left him and went away. **Mark 12:1-12***

Jesus sits in the midst of the crowd. Once again they have gathered around Him, seeking to be near Him, seeking to hear His words. They close in around Him, sitting close. He doesn't seem to mind. Instead, He continues to teach them, His parables bringing further conviction of the Pharisees.

Because they fear the crowds and because they see that Jesus is calling them out, indicting them before the crowd, the Pharisees try another tack today. They send spies into the crowd. Spies to blend in. Spies to fake sincerity and affect genuine interest in His wisdom and teaching. But they are there hoping to catch Him speaking words against the government and therefore bring Him to the authorities, to Caesar, and finally rid Jerusalem of this Jesus who sees the hearts of the chief priests and scribes and calls them out on what He sees.

But Jesus perceives this. Even as the crowd presses around Him, He sees each of their hearts as plainly as if it were just Him and that one person, not the crowd. When they pose their question, hoping finally to catch Him and rid Jerusalem of Him, He answers them truthfully, boldly, and as always, without hesitation.

At His answer these spies seemingly become like the crowd surrounding Him. Hearing His words, they, too, marvel at His answer, at the Truth in His words. In His presence they fall silent, no longer out to get rid of Him but wanting to draw near to Him. At least for this moment.

In their silent surrender, in this moment, I realize there is no pretending in the presence of Jesus. He sees our hearts and He knows if we're faking it. When it comes to a relationship with Jesus, you are either all in or not in at all. You cannot have one foot in the world and the other in heaven. You cannot claim loyalty to both and you certainly cannot seek the acceptance of both. They too often contradict each other, don't they?

Certainly God's ways are not the world's ways (Isaiah 55:8-9). Where the world preaches self — self-centeredness, selfishness, self-made dreams, self-made men, legacies and empires — God calls His people to be selfless, to be servants, to be humble, and to be sacrificial. He doesn't expect us to be perfect, but He does expect us to reflect His love, His hope, and His grace to others.

We can live in this world. We can adhere to the laws of this world. We can render to this world what belongs to this world. But we will never truly be citizens of this world if we claim to be heirs with Jesus. By that relationship we become instead citizens of heaven. We become sojourners in this world. There can be no dual citizenship. We must choose.

I choose Jesus.

Prayer

Dear Jesus, thank you for your example and for revealing the Truth. Thank you for your invitation to sit with you, to listen to you, and to learn from you. Remind me, Lord, that this world is not my home and that I am holy because you are holy. Thank you for giving me your Spirit and your strength so that I can stand strong in a world whose ways focus on self.

Additional Scripture for Reflection

Isaiah 55:8-9

Philippians 1:27-30

Matthew 20:25-28

Day 32: A Change of Heart?

Then he began to tell the people this parable: "A man planted a vineyard, leased it to tenant farmers, and went on a journey for a long time. When harvest time came, he sent a slave to the tenants so that they would give him his portion of the crop. However, the tenants beat his slave and sent him away empty-handed. So he sent another slave. They beat this one too, treated him outrageously, and sent him away empty-handed. So he sent still a third. They even wounded this one, and threw him out. Then the owner of the vineyard said, 'What should I do? I will send my one dear son; perhaps they will respect him.' But when the tenants saw him, they said to one another, 'This is the heir; let's kill him so the inheritance will be ours!' So they threw him out of the vineyard and killed him. What then will the owner of the vineyard do to them? He will come and destroy those tenants and give the vineyard to others." When the people heard this, they said, "May this never happen!" But Jesus looked straight at them and said, "Then what is the meaning of that which is written: 'The stone the builders rejected has become the cornerstone'? Everyone who falls on this stone will be broken to pieces, and the one on whom it falls will be crushed." Then the experts in the law and the chief priests wanted to arrest him that very hour, because they realized he had told this parable against them. But they were afraid of the people.

Then they watched him carefully and sent spies who pretended to be sincere. They wanted to take advantage of what he might say so that they could deliver him up to the authority and jurisdiction of the governor. Thus they asked him, "Teacher, we know that you speak and teach correctly, and show no partiality, but teach the way of God in accordance with the truth. Is it right for us to pay the tribute tax to Caesar or not?" But Jesus perceived their deceit and said to them, "Show me a denarius. Whose image and inscription are on it?" They said, "Caesar's." So he said to them, "Then give to Caesar the things that are Caesar's, and to God the things that are God's." Thus they were unable in the presence of the people to trap him with his own words. And stunned by his answer, they fell silent. **Luke 20:9-26**

Watching Jesus teach the crowds in the temple is always amazing. The crowds come because they are drawn by His words as well as His presence. They are drawn to Him and their rapt expressions are a contrast to the skeptical expressions worn by the chief priests, scribes, and elders. Their skepticism is tinged with disdain and judgment, and I can almost see their minds turning over ideas for ways to deal with Jesus' teaching and popularity. Of course, Jesus makes no effort to smooth their ruffled feathers. In fact, His parables almost always prick at their prideful hearts again and again. Because of this, I marvel at their stubborn refusal to even consider who Jesus truly is. Why would they rather continue in their anger and judgment instead of exploring whether He is who He says He is?

Despite our differences in how we see Jesus, I can empathize with these religious leaders. It's never easy to be singled out in a crowd when the person singling you out points to the worst in you rather than the best. In each encounter between Jesus and the Pharisees and chief priests, Jesus focuses on their flaws as He points out how wrong they are in their ways of thinking about themselves and others. As well, Jesus criticizes how they treat the crowds. Maybe you've been treated similarly in front of others — friends, family, colleagues. You feel belittled, humiliated, angry, defensive. You deserve to be treated better. After all, none of us want to hear someone catalog our worst qualities. But that's exactly what happens between Jesus and the religious leaders.

But that's why Jesus came, isn't it?

He didn't come to lavish us with praise or tell us how good we are while overlooking the hidden (and not-so-hidden) flawed parts of us. He came because he knows our hearts. We may be able to convince ourselves that we are good enough even though we sometimes get angry with our children or our spouse. We may be able to rationalize telling a small lie or justifying our impatience or thinking of ourselves better than we deserve because we do good deeds in other parts of our lives. Jesus sees through all of it. And I don't know about you, but I don't always like that side of Jesus. I don't like the way He shows up to point out when I'm doing things wrong. I don't like the way He pierces the grudge in my heart with the truth of needing to forgive those who have hurt me. I don't like having to admit when I'm wrong.

As I watch the Pharisees, scribes, and other religious leaders, I see myself in them as they bristle at Jesus' words. His teachings underscore the wicked motivations of their words and deeds and reflects what's in their hearts and they don't appreciate that. Today's parable creates no different response from them; they are done enduring these moments and they are tiring of his popularity. But they, too, see the awe in the crowd, and they sense the way people respond to Jesus so they do not dare act on their desire to seize Jesus.

Instead, once again, they attempt to manipulate the circumstances to try and create the grounds and opportunity to arrest Him. They rely on spies to act as followers and question Him about paying tribute to Caesar instead of God. Again, I marvel at their actions and wonder how it is they think this time they are going to outsmart Him. Equally confusing to me is that these encounters with Jesus do nothing to change their hearts or their perspective. He reads their hearts every single time, and yet they do not stop to question how it is He sees through their efforts and actions. They do not pause in their desire to seize Him even long enough to consider He may well be the Messiah for whom they have waited.

The irony in these moments is that the Pharisees and chief priests believe they are testing Jesus, but it is in fact Jesus who is testing them. But unlike His adversaries who are seeking to do Him harm, Jesus is seeking to *change* their hearts. Each of these parables and teachings, each of these encounters, is one more opportunity Jesus affords them to admit their need for God. Jesus doesn't want them to continue in a cursory relationship with God like what the Pharisees are used to - giving only what is required, singing their own praises for doing so, praying loudly for others to hear, considering the Law and not the God who put the Law in place. Jesus wants more than this, not for Him, but for *them*.

Unfortunately, they don't see that. They refuse to see it. They are too focused on themselves and how Jesus makes them look before the crowds and how He is upending their carefully curated routines. It's never comfortable to consider making changes in our lives. But Jesus is not concerned with our comfort. He cares about our hearts. Jesus is not concerned with only our lives in this world. He cares about our eternal lives. Jesus knows that to reject Him as the Pharisees continually do will ultimately lead to our being rejected by Him.

And that's not why He came.

He came so that we may have life, and have it abundantly (John 10:10) and eternally, both through Him and with Him.

Prayer

Dear Jesus, it's not always easy for me to admit how much I need You or let You bring about the change in me that I truly need. It is far easier for me to be comfortable with the habits I've created for myself than to trust You with *all* of me. Thank you for not giving up on me and for coming into this world so that I can have abundant life. Please continue to show me what abundant life looks like from Your eternal perspective and not my worldly one.

Additional Scripture for Reflection

Isaiah 55:8-9

Philippians 1:27-30

Matthew 20:25-28

Day 31: Selective Hearing When God Speaks

*Now some Sadducees (who contend that there is no resurrection) came to him. They asked him, "Teacher, Moses wrote for us that **if a man's brother dies leaving** a wife but **no children, that man must marry the widow and father children for his brother.** Now there were seven brothers. The first one married a woman and died without children. The second and then the third married her, and in this same way all seven died, leaving no children. Finally the woman died too. In the resurrection, therefore, whose wife will the woman be? For all seven had married her."*

*So Jesus said to them, "The people of this age marry and are given in marriage. But those who are regarded as worthy to share in that age and in the resurrection from the dead neither marry nor are given in marriage. In fact, they can no longer die because they are equal to angels and are sons of God, since they are sons of the resurrection. But even Moses revealed that the dead are raised in the passage abut the bush, where he calls the Lord **the God of Abraham and the God of Isaac and the God of Jacob.** Now he is not God of the dead, but of the living, for all live before him." Then some of the experts in the law answered, "Teacher, you have spoken well! For they did not dare any longer to ask him anything. **Luke 20:27-40***

I cannot help but wonder what Jesus hopes to accomplish here in Jerusalem. Certainly as God, He must know nothing He does, nothing He says, will change the hearts of the Pharisees and Sadducees. And yet He pursues them passionately, relentlessly, with parable after parable, responding to their questions and their trickery with boldness and truth.

And though it silences them for the moment, it doesn't seem to change them. At least not noticeably. Not outwardly. They may be reluctant to ask Him any other questions at the moment, but they don't seem convinced. Once again, it's unlikely Jesus has changed their minds, and I can't help but wonder why.

They sit in the presence of Jesus. They hear His words. But rather than absorb them, rather than accept them like the rest of the crowd, they pick and choose what they hear. They pick and choose what they believe.

In fact, they actually take part of what God said in His word and try to use it against Him. They don't believe in the resurrection, but they want Jesus to explain it to them. But Jesus doesn't give in to their trickery. Rather than explaining the resurrection to them, Jesus tells them that God is not the God of the dead, but the God of the living, including Abraham, Isaac and Jacob. Alongside what Moses had to say about brothers and wives, Moses also testified to this: that to God, all are alive.

This isn't what they want to hear.

In most of their run-ins with Jesus, the Pharisees and Sadducees cherry pick the parts of God's word that works to their benefit, that works to their planned end of trapping Jesus. Their only focus, their only concern is ridding Jerusalem of Jesus.

Although they perceive the parables are about them and the parables testify against them, they choose not to hear those words.

They listen, but they do not heed. They do not hear. When it comes to what Jesus has to say, they have selective hearing. Sitting here in Jerusalem listening to this interaction between Jesus and the Sadducees, I hear the promise of resurrection and eternal life. But I also hear conviction because I have been a Sadducee. I have been a Pharisee. I have practiced selective hearing.

Following Jesus, being in a relationship with the Creator, is not easy. It challenges the status quo. It goes against the things of the world. It requires boldness and truth and courage. It requires us to heed His words. And so, sometimes it is easier to ignore what Jesus says than to hear His words, or to heed His commands, or to respond to what He requests of me.

Like this group of Sadducees and Pharisees, I haven't spoken up for those without a voice because it was too risky to my comfortable life.

With my selective hearing, I haven't always loved my neighbor as myself because I didn't like or agree with my neighbor even though that's not part of the criteria for love.

Like these Sadducees and Pharisees, I have struggled more often than I can count to give up control of my plans, my dreams, my life to Jesus because I sometimes think I know better what I need.

Because of my selective hearing, I haven't forgiven others right away even though I have been forgiven because in my mind what they did is so much worse than anything I've done.

I haven't stood up for truth or shined God's light in my small corner of the world because I have been too afraid of what people will say about me. Like the Pharisees, I've been too afraid I might lose my reputation, some of my friends, my perceived status, or my comfort here in this world.

But as I continue this journey with Jesus around Jerusalem, as we approach what is coming, drawing closer to Golgotha, I cannot help but look Jesus in the eyes and acknowledge sometimes I refuse to hear Him when He calls my name. I cannot help but repent and seek His grace, His forgiveness and His second chance. Again. Right now, right here. In Jerusalem.

The cross looms in the distance. Jesus' death is inevitable.

But right now, here in Jerusalem, His life is vibrant, passionate, laser-focused on the message of His Kingdom. Love flows from Him and through Him and I count myself blessed to be here, in His company, in Jerusalem. And I rise to the challenge I read in His life. I rise to the call to be a light, to be a vessel of His light, to be a bearer of His message. I rise to the challenge to hear everything He says with His life. Not just the things that are easy for me to do. Everything.

Yes, today, I hear everything. Today, I hear every word His heart speaks to mine.

Prayer

Dear Jesus, thank you for letting me take this journey with you and for showing me who you are. Even though your words and your life challenge me and highlight the areas in my life and attitude that need more of you and less of me, your love and your grace and your mercy invite me to abide in you and trust in you. That the more I surrender my will and my life to you, the more change I will see in my life. Thank you for your patience that allows me to grow and to stumble and to begin again. Help me today not only to hear your words but to heed them, too.

Additional Scripture for Reflection

James 1:19-25

Matthew 5:13-16

Psalm 139:23-24

A Day of Reading and Reflection

Additional Scripture for Reflection

Genesis 17:1-7, 15-16

When Abram was ninety-nine years old, the Lord appeared to him and said, "I am the Sovereign God. Walk before me and be blameless. Then I will confirm my covenant between me and you, and I will give you a multitude of descendants."

Abram bowed down with his face to the ground, and God said to him, "As for me, this is my covenant with you: You will be the father of a multitude of nations. No longer will your name be Abram. Instead, your name will be Abraham because I will make you the father of a multitude of nations. I will make you extremely fruitful. I will make nations of you, and kings will descend from you. I will confirm my covenant as a perpetual covenant between me and you. It will extend to your descendants after you throughout their generations. I will be your God and the God of your descendants after you."

Then God said to Abraham, "As for your wife, you must no longer call her Sarai; Sarah will be her name. I will bless her and will give you a son through her. I will bless her and she will become a mother of nations. Kings of countries will come from her!"

Psalm 22:23-31

You loyal followers of the LORD, praise him.

All you descendants of Jacob, honor him.

All you descendants of Israel, stand in awe of him.

For he did not despise or detest the suffering of the oppressed.

He did not ignore him;

when he cried out to him, he responded.

You are the reason I offer praise in the great assembly;

I will fulfill my promises before the Lord's loyal followers.

Let the oppressed eat and be filled.

Let those who seek his help praise the LORD.

May you live forever!

Let all the people of the earth acknowledge the LORD and turn to him.

Let all the nations worship you.

For the LORD is king

and rules over the nations.

All the thriving people of the earth will join the celebration and worship;

all those who are descending into the grave will bow before him,

including those who cannot preserve their lives.

A whole generation will serve him;

they will tell the next generation about the Lord.

They will come and tell about his saving deeds;

they will tell a future generation what he has accomplished.

Romans 4:13-25

*For the promise to Abraham or to his descendants that he would inherit the world was not fulfilled through the law, but through the righteousness that comes by faith. For if they become heirs by the law, faith is empty and the promise is nullified. For the law brings wrath, because where there is no law there is no transgression either. For this reason it is by faith so that it may be by grace, with the result that the promise may be certain to all the descendants—not only to those who are under the law, but also to those who have the faith of Abraham, who is the father of us all (as it is written, "**I have made you the father of many nations**"). He is our father in the presence of God whom he believed—the God who makes the dead alive and summons the things that do not yet exist as though they already do. Against hope Abraham believed in hope with the result that he became **the father of many nations** according to the pronouncement, "**so will your descendants be**." Without being weak in faith, he considered his own body as dead (because he was about one hundred years old) and the deadness of Sarah's womb. He did not waver in unbelief about the promise of God but was strengthened in faith, giving glory to God. He was fully convinced that what God promised he was* *also able to do. So indeed it was credited to Abraham as righteousness.*

*But the statement **it was credited to him** was not written only for Abraham's sake, but also for our sake, to whom it will be credited, those who believe in the one who raised Jesus our Lord from the dead. He was given over because of our transgressions and was raised for the sake of our justification.*

Mark 8:31-38

Then Jesus began to teach them that the Son of Man must suffer many things and be rejected by the elders, chief priests, and experts in the law, and be killed, and after three days rise again. He spoke openly about this. So Peter took him aside and began to rebuke him. But after turning and looking at his disciples, he rebuked Peter and said, "Get behind me, Satan. You are not setting your mind on God's interests, but on man's."

Then Jesus called the crowd, along with his disciples, and said to them, "If anyone wants to become my follower, he must deny himself, take up his cross, and follow me. For whoever wants to save his life will lose it, but whoever loses his life because of me and because of the gospel will save it. For what benefit is it for a person to gain the whole world, yet forfeit his life? What can a person give in exchange for his life? For if anyone is ashamed of me and my words in this adulterous and sinful generation, the Son of Man will also be ashamed of him when he comes in the glory of his Father with the holy angels."

Day 30: What Am I Missing?

*Now when the Pharisees heard that he had silenced the Sadducees, they assembled together. And one of them, an expert in religious law, asked him a question to test him: "Teacher, which commandment in the law is the greatest?" Jesus said to him, "'**Love the Lord your God with all your heart, with all your soul, and with all your mind.**' This is the first and greatest commandment. The second is like it: '**Love your neighbor as yourself.**' All the law and the prophets depend on these two commandments."*

While the Pharisees were assembled, Jesus asked them a question: "What do you think about the Christ? Whose son is he?" They said, "The son of David." He said to them, "How then does David by the Spirit call him 'Lord,' saying,

> *"'**The Lord said to my lord,**
>
> *"**Sit at my right hand,**
>
> *until I put your enemies under your feet?'?**

If David then calls him 'Lord', how can he be his son?" No one was able to answer him a word, and from that day on no one dared to question him any longer. **Matthew 22:34-46**

When it comes to tricking Jesus, to stopping Jesus, to silencing Jesus, the Pharisees are as relentless in trying to catch and convict Him as Jesus is in trying to catch and convict them. Except where the Pharisees' on-going efforts to convict Christ are focused on doing away with Him by killing Him, Jesus' continued efforts involving these religious leaders is focused on providing them with life, His life, eternal life.

On this journey to Jerusalem, I sit beside Jesus and watch. And wonder.

I wonder how the Pharisees can sit in the physical presence of Jesus and not see in Him what His disciples see in Him.

I wonder how the Pharisees feel in these moments. Does anything He says or does stir their hearts or bend them toward Jesus, toward truth, or toward heaven even a little bit?

I wonder what the crowd thinks, witnessing these exchanges time and again. Do they understand the importance of these moments or understand the motivation of the religious leaders? Do they understand why Jesus is doing what He is doing? Do they care?

I wonder why Jesus doesn't simply write these men off as a waste of His time. He has so little time left, why does He choose to spend it like this? Why does He continue to engage with this group of unbelievers, and not merely engage with them, but pursue them?

But that is the very nature of Jesus. He has spent His ministry with sinners in need of grace. He has dined with tax collectors and sat in the presence of prostitutes. He has touched lepers and embraced children and sought out other lesser-than people. He has corrected and admonished and convicted and forgiven. His words have been sometimes kind, sometimes harsh, but always, always His words are loving.

And yet, they miss it. The Pharisees miss who Jesus is. Even when He speaks directly to them about who their Savior will be, they cannot see Him sitting here before them. Even when He quotes the Scriptures and claims it is fulfilled before them, they refuse to believe. They are so intent on their own purposes and their own pursuits, they miss the wonder, they miss this incredible gift set before them, they miss the miracle right before their eyes.

A familiar twinge winds its way into my consciousness and into my heart. It is conviction. It is a call to examine my own response to Jesus. To examine my own motivations. To examine and remove the log from my own eye even as I sit here and worry about the speck in the Pharisees' eyes.

I can't help but wonder how many blessings I've missed because I was too preoccupied with being right or being heard or being acknowledged for my efforts.

I can't help but wonder how many miracles I've overlooked because I had something to prove or was walking down the wrong road.

I can't help but wonder how many times I've not seen Jesus sitting right in front of me because He didn't look anything like what I expected or I didn't like what He was saying.

I can't help but wonder how many times I've been an enemy of Christ without realizing it, a little bit like Peter, zealous one moment, messing up the next, and a little bit like the Pharisees, overly proud and self-reliant because I've decided Jesus isn't who He says He is.

I can't help but wonder how many times I've been given the opportunity to offer hope, to provide encouragement, to change the world, to change one heart, to change one life, and missed it?

Here in Jerusalem with Jesus right now, sitting at His dusty feet as I've done each day, I take this opportunity to peer inside my heart, to rearrange my priorities, to realize my need of this Savior, every day. Sometimes, on more challenging days, every minute.

And I ask myself, *So what are you going to do about these things?* Because that is what this journey is really about. What will I do with these truths? What will I do with this Jesus? What will I let Jesus do with me?

And, most importantly, I can't help but wonder what we are going to do together, this Jesus and me, to change this world? *His* world.

Prayer

Dear Jesus, thank you for pursuing me and for being a God of second chances when I mess up or miss the first one. Thank you for redeeming my failures and for inviting me to help you change your world. But mostly, thank you for loving me the way I am and helping me become who you created me to be.

Additional Scripture for Reflection

Mark 2:13-17

Luke 19:1-10

Romans 5:1-11

Day 29: You Call That Love?

*Then Jesus said to the crowds and to his disciples,
"The scribes and the Pharisees sit on Moses' seat, so do
and observe whatever they tell you, but not the works they
do. For they preach, but do not practice. They tie up
heavy burdens, hard to bear, and lay them on people's
shoulders, but they themselves are not willing to move
them with their finger. They do all their deeds to be seen
by others. For they make their phylacteries broad and
their fringes long, and they love the place of honor at
feasts and the best seats in the synagogues and greetings
in the marketplaces and being called rabbi by others. But
you are not to be called rabbi, for you have one teacher,
and you are all brothers. And call no man your father on
earth, for you have one Father, who is in heaven. Neither
be called instructors, for you have one instructor, the
Christ. The greatest among you shall be your servant.
Whoever exalts himself will be humbled, and whoever
humbles himself will be exalted.*

*"But woe to you, scribes and Pharisees, hypocrites!
For you shut the kingdom of heaven in people's faces. For
you neither enter yourselves nor allow those who would
enter to go in. Woe to you, scribes and Pharisees,
hypocrites! For you travel across sea and land to make a
single proselyte, and when he becomes a proselyte, you
make him twice as much a child of hell as yourselves.*

*"Woe to you, blind guides, who say, 'If anyone
swears by the temple, it is nothing, but if anyone swears*

by the gold of the temple, he is bound by his oath.' You blind fools! For which is greater, the gold or the temple that has made the gold sacred? And you say, 'If anyone swears by the altar, it is nothing, but if anyone swears by the gift that is on the altar, he is bound by his oath.' You blind men! For which is greater, the gift or the altar that makes the gift sacred? So whoever swears by the altar swears by it and by everything on it. And whoever swears by the temple swears by it and by him who dwells in it. And whoever swears by heaven swears by the throne of God and by him who sits upon it.

"Woe to you, scribes and Pharisees, hypocrites! For you tithe mint and dill and cumin, and have neglected the weightier matters of the law: justice and mercy and faithfulness. These you ought to have done, without neglecting the others. You blind guides, straining out a gnat and swallowing a camel!

"Woe to you, scribes and Pharisees, hypocrites! For you clean the outside of the cup and the plate, but inside they are full of greed and self-indulgence. You blind Pharisee! First clean the inside of the cup and the plate, that the outside also may be clean.

"Woe to you, scribes and Pharisees, hypocrites! For you are like whitewashed tombs, which outwardly appear beautiful, but within are full of dead people's bones and all uncleanness. So you also outwardly appear righteous to others, but within you are full of hypocrisy and lawlessness.

Then Jesus said to the crowds and to his disciples, "The experts in the law and the Pharisees sit on Moses' seat. Therefore pay attention to what they tell you and do it. But do not do what they do, for they do not practice what they teach. They tie up heavy loads, hard to carry, and put them on men's shoulders, but they themselves are not willing even to lift a finger to move them. They do all their deeds to be seen by people, for they make their phylacteries wide and their tassels long. They love the place of honor at banquets and the best seats in the synagogues and elaborate greetings in the marketplaces and to have people call them 'Rabbi'. But you are not to be called 'Rabbi', for you have one Teacher and you are all brothers. And call no one your 'father' on earth, for you have one Father, who is in heaven. Nor are you to be called 'teacher', for you have one Teacher, the Christ. The greatest among you will be your servant. And whoever exalts himself will be humbled, and whoever humbles himself will be exalted.

"But woe to you, experts in the law and you Pharisees, hypocrites! You keep locking people out of the kingdom of heaven! For you neither enter nor permit those trying to enter to go in.

"Woe to you, experts in the law and you Pharisees, hypocrites! You cross land and sea to make one convert, and when you get one, you make him twice as much a child of hell as yourselves!

"Woe to you, blind guides, who say, 'Whoever swears by the temple is bound by nothing. But whoever swears by the gold of the temple is bound by the oath.'

Blind fools! Which is greater, the gold or the temple that makes the gold sacred? And, 'Whoever swears by the altar is bound by nothing. But if anyone swears by the gift on it he is bound by the oath'. You are blind! For which is greater, the gift or the altar that makes the gift sacred? So whoever swears by the altar swears by it and by everything on it. And whoever swears by the temple swears by it and the one who dwells in it. And whoever swears by heaven swears by the throne of God and the one who sits on it.

"Woe to you, experts in the law and you Pharisees, hypocrites! You give a tenth of mint, dill, and cumin, yet you neglect what is more important in the law—justice, mercy, and faithfulness! You should have done these things without neglecting the others. Blind guides! You strain out a gnat yet swallow a camel!

"Woe to you, experts in the law and you Pharisees, hypocrites! You clean the outside of the cup and the dish, but inside they are full of greed and self-indulgence. Blind Pharisee! First clean the inside of the cup, so that the outside may become clean too!

"Woe to you, experts in the law and you Pharisees, hypocrites! You are like whitewashed tombs that look beautiful on the outside but inside are full of the bones of the dead and of everything unclean. In the same way, on the outside you look righteous to people, but inside you are full of hypocrisy and lawlessness.

"Woe to you, experts in the law and you Pharisees, hypocrites! You build tombs for the prophets and decorate

the graves of the righteous. And you say, 'If we had lived in the days of our ancestors, we would not have participated with them in shedding the blood of the prophets'. By saying this you testify against yourselves that you are descendants of those who murdered the prophets. Fill up then the measure of your ancestors! You snakes, you offspring of vipers! How will you escape being condemned to hell?

"For this reason I am sending you prophets and wise men and experts in the law, some of whom you will kill and crucify, and some you will flog in your synagogues and pursue from town to town, so that on you will come all the righteous blood shed on earth, from the blood of righteous Abel to the blood of Zechariah son of Barachiah, whom you murdered between the temple and the altar. I tell you the truth, this generation will be held responsible for all these things!

*"O Jerusalem, Jerusalem, you who kill the prophets and stone those who are sent to you! How often I have longed to gather your children together as a hen gathers her chicks under her wings, but you would have none of it! Look, your house is left to you desolate! For I tell you, you will not see me from now until you say, '****Blessed is the one who comes in the name of the Lord!****'" Matthew 23:1-39*

There are no hidden meanings in Jesus' words today. There are some metaphors, but this list of grievances against the

Pharisees and scribes is long and bluntly stated. And Jesus' anger is as plain, as obvious, as His condemning words.

It is righteous anger to be sure, but even so, I shift uncomfortably. I pull back from Him a little bit this morning. This is not the sweet, easy-going, loving Jesus that I am used to. This Jesus is still loving, but He is also harsh, condemning, and zealous in His attack on the Pharisees, in His attack on sin.

I am not privy to the Pharisees' or scribes' reactions to Jesus in this moment. But given their desire to stop Him, their whispers about wanting to destroy Him, and the confrontational interactions I've witnessed in their previous interactions with Jesus to this point here in Jerusalem, I can easily imagine their sense of outrage, their indignation, and their anger undulating just beneath the surface of their seemingly placid faces. How can they not feel outraged and insulted at this most recent barrage of barbs cutting them down? Jesus is calling them out boldly in front of the crowds. Never has this group of religious elite seemed more human to me than in this moment. Jesus reveals their sinfulness and puts their hypocrisy on display for all to see. In them, I see weakness and fear and insecurity. Their facades are being attacked and the cracks are obvious as they glare around at Jesus, His disciples, and the crowd.

As I witness this intense moment, I am reminded just how much God hates sin. Sin not only angers Him but it sometimes motivates Him to destroy. In the name of sin He has destroyed rulers, whole towns, armies, and even the very world He created.

Indeed, this is a side of Jesus with which I definitely am not comfortable. I like to focus on His grace, His unconditional love, His forgiveness, His redemption. But watching Him today, I recall that the reason for His grace, His forgiveness, and His redemption is the sin that angers Him so. Underneath all of His anger remains His love: tough love, unrelenting love, unconditional love.

Even so, this aspect of His love causes me to tremble. It causes me to look away and even move away, even if only slightly from my place beside Him.

Because in this moment, His love doesn't seem so unconditional, does it? It seems hinged upon the Pharisees finally relenting, finally acknowledging their hypocrisy, finally admitting their unbelief, and finally, at long last, confessing their sin. Regardless of what it appears to be, His love is not. Not really.

From my spot near Jesus, I can see how wrong that supposition is. I can see the love, and the pain, in His eyes even as they flash with anger. He wants the Pharisees, the scribes, the Sadducees, and the whole of this crowd to enter into His Kingdom. In fact, He wants it more than they do. His anger is as much imploring as it is condemning. It is as much an invitation, even a plea, as it is a conviction.

He loves them as much as, and probably more than, they appear to hate Him.

Because their anger, like that of Jesus, boils, too, right now, doesn't it? In every encounter, I watch their roiling, defensive anger. It's an anger that seems to match the Savior's, except their anger is not motivated by love. Their anger is motivated by self-preservation, by their need for power, by their pride, and by their need to mask their humanity, with all its imperfections, and, most of all, their sinfulness.

Oh, how I have been there, like these rulers. I have experienced that burning anger, that burning *defensive* anger, motivated by the fear of being seen, the fear of being known for who I am and what I've done. And it doesn't stop just because you relent and admit your need for Jesus or your need for forgiveness. Being forgiven, being in a relationship with Jesus, doesn't keep me from messing up. It doesn't stop me from hurting others. It doesn't mean I make the right choice every time. Because of these imperfections and in spite of my relationship with Jesus, I still experience that all-to-familiar burning defensive anger behind which I want to hide my flaws and brokenness in the presence of my Savior.

Being a follower of Jesus doesn't mean I don't experience this familiar anger every time I am faced with my screw ups or for I'm seen in my sinfulness and weakness. My desire for self-preservation and my self-centeredness remain, though they continue growing smaller as my love and admitted need for Jesus grow larger, even now, as I sit uncomfortably in His presence.

Oh, how I wish I could whisper this truth to the Pharisees. How I wish I could pull them aside and help them see who Jesus is and what He wants from them. He wants their hearts. He wants their lives. In return, He will make them greater than they've ever been. Just not in the way they want, that they are trying to create for themselves. It will be so much better than you can imagine, I want to tell them.

But they won't listen. They won't hear me.

So, I'll whisper it to myself. Over and over, again and again. It won't be easy. It won't be easy. It won't look anything like you think or hope it will. But it will be worth it. And it will be better. So much better.

I edge closer to Jesus again. Comfortable and content to be uncomfortable by His nearness to me.

Prayer

Dear Jesus, sometimes I choose to ignore your anger at sin or I refuse to heed the conviction of your Spirit for my wrongs — my need to ask others' forgiveness, for hurtful words, for defensive anger. Thank you that you offer to cast my sins as far as the East is from the West if I will come to you and confess them to you. And thank you that as I release my sins and my darkness, as I surrender my selfishness to you, you pour out your amazing grace and pour over me your incredible blessings.

Additional Scripture for Reflection

Micah 6:8

2 Peter 3:3-9

Psalm 139:7-12

Day 28: I Will If You Will

*Then he sat down opposite the offering box, and watched the crowd putting coins into it. Many rich people were throwing in large amounts. And a poor widow came and put in two small copper coins, worth less than a penny. He called his disciples and said to them, "I tell you the truth, this poor widow has put more into the offering box than all the others. For they all gave out of their wealth. But she, out of her poverty, put in what she had to live on, everything she had." **Mark 12:41-44**

How strange it is sitting here with Jesus today. We sit in the synagogue and relax as people pass by bringing their offerings. The offering box is in the front of the synagogue and what you give can be seen by all. It doesn't really seem all that interesting, sitting here people watching, given how much energy usually surrounds Jesus. It is a strange lull, especially after His recent confrontations with the religious leaders.

And that's when it happens. As I drift into a bit of a lull of my own, relaxed and mostly disengaged, the energy changes. I sense it immediately, but I don't know why. I look around, searching for an answer, and my eyes meet His. Although I teeter on the edge of feeling embarrassed, almost chagrined, Jesus looks at me with love, in His eyes an invitation to come and know. He calls us over to help us understand what He already knows. Once more, Jesus sees something the rest of us miss. He calls us closer to Himself and shares what He sees, what He knows, with us in His familiar whisper.

In this moment, what He knows has something to do with a poor widow who has just placed her offering in the box. He points her out to us and I wonder if she feels His eyes on her. If she feels all of the disciples staring at her, watching her as she leaves, she doesn't show it. She doesn't glance back, nor does she shrink into herself. It is her sense of herself, her sense of God, and her faith that give her a bold presence of quiet confidence that seems deeply rooted to God, and I can see it in Jesus' eyes that she does. She has a deep love and reverence for God among this gathering of rich tithers that makes her stand out to me even though she seems invisible to the surrounding crowd.

Jesus tells us that she has given out of her poverty, out of her need, but because of her quiet confidence and trust in God, she looks anything but poor to me despite her worn and weary appearance and tired steps.

Jesus tells us that she has given everything she had, which means she has nothing left, but she looks anything but needy to me. Though her steps belie a life of hard work and her clothes reflect wear, I sense a beauty radiating from deep within her, a richness of heart and spirit and faith.

Jesus tells us that she has given more than those who gave amounts several times more than what she gave, but she looks richer than they do to me.

As I sit beside Jesus and listen to Him talk about this woman with such love and reverence, once again I am reminded that God doesn't see people the way we do, *the way I do*. He doesn't see *me* the way the world does, or the way *I see myself*. He doesn't look at how much money I have or how much money I can give. He doesn't look at the job I do or how successful I appear to be. He doesn't look at my standing in the community or what others think about me.

He looks at the heart. He looks at *my* heart. He looks at what motivates me. He looks at what influences my actions. He looks at what informs my thoughts and my decisions. He looks at my heart; even more, He *examines* my heart. He *cares* about my heart.

And I cannot help but wonder if, when Jesus looks around my heart, does He see himself reflected there? Is there enough room for Him in there? Or do I need to clean some things out? Like in the deepest recesses where I let fear stay and creep around unchecked, or where I let sin and unforgiveness linger a little bit longer than they should before addressing them, or where I let anger lurk like a prowling lion or pride hide until I think I need it or envy fester like an open sore?

Yes, I need to clean these things out for Jesus to have the room He needs. But even more, I need to clean these things out and make Him room because I *need Him*. I need Him to guide me and to remind me of my worth. I need Him to refine me and resurrect me, to resurrect this heart that has become dead to wonder, forgiveness, and the sacred within the brokenness of this world. In fact, it's not only time to clean these things out, it's time to put them in the collection box. It's time to give them to Jesus, to place them in His hands so that He has a place in my heart. So that, as much as it's possible by failing and trying again and again, He has the *only* place in my heart.

The widow gave all she had out of her poverty. Perhaps it is time for me to give all of me out of my brokenness. Perhaps it is time for me to trust Jesus with my life, like this widow so clearly does. To trust Him with my whole life and not just the parts that are easy to relinquish control of. Can I trust Him with my whole life? That is the question He is asking me today as He points out the widow's offering to me.

Can I?

Will I?

Do I?

He already knows the answer. After all, He can see my heart. He *knows* my heart. But even so, I will tell Him. I will give Him my answer. I will give Him my life.

Yes, Jesus, I will trust you with my life.

I can. I will. I do. So long as you help me, Lord.

So long as you help me.

Prayer

Dear Jesus, what do you see when you look at my heart? Search my heart, Lord, and root out all the things that clutter and crowd it: worry, fear, past hurts, anger, unresolved conflicts. Bring them into the Light, your Light, and help me to address them so that there is more room for you in my heart today. Today, Jesus, I give you my heart, my life, my all.

Additional Scripture for Reflection

1 Samuel 16:1-13

Romans 12:1-3

John 15:1-8

Day 27: What Did I Get Myself Into?

Now as Jesus was going out of the temple courts, one of his disciples said to him, "Teacher, look at these tremendous stones and buildings!" Jesus said to him, "Do you see these great buildings? Not one stone will be left on another. All will be torn down!"

So while he was sitting on the Mount of Olives opposite the temple, Peter, James, John, and Andrew asked him privately, "Tell us, when will these things happen? And what will be the sign that all these things are about to take place?" Jesus began to say to them, "Watch out that no one misleads you. Many will come in my name, saying, 'I am he', and they will mislead many. When you hear of wars and rumors of wars, do not be alarmed. These things must happen, but the end is still to come. For nation will rise up in arms against nation, and kingdom against kingdom. There will be earthquakes in various places, and there will be famines. These are but the beginning of birth pains.

"You must watch out for yourselves. You will be handed over to councils and beaten in the synagogues. You will stand before governors and kings because of me, as a witness to them. First the gospel must be preached to all nations. When they arrest you and hand you over for trial, do not worry about what to speak. But say whatever is given to you at that time, for it is not you speaking, but

the Holy Spirit. Brother will hand over brother to death, and a father his child. Children will rise against parents and have them put to death. You will be hated by everyone because of my name. But the one who endures to the end will be saved. **Mark 13:1-13**

Today is one of those days when being a disciple, being a follower of Jesus, leaves me scratching my head and reconsidering my choice to be a part of Jesus' crew and His Jerusalem journey. There is no feel-good exchange and Jesus' words don't offer a whole lot of hope.

Following Jesus around Jerusalem isn't so bad when He is taking on the Pharisees and Sadducees and challenging the status quo or when He is teaching His disciples important lessons about fig trees and widows. But this? This is definitely a difficult moment to be a part of. It's an incredibly difficult lesson to absorb. And, honestly, I'd really rather not have to.

One of the disciples offers a seemingly innocuous observation about the beautiful buildings surrounding the temple. A comment about the wonderful stones that created such beautiful buildings. Jesus' response seems strange, incongruous even. He addresses not the beauty but the destruction of this beauty.

It's not all that surprising then that the next thing the disciples ask Him is when. When is all of this going to happen? And how will they know it's about to happen? I don't know why they want to know these things, but as I sit here on the Mount of Olives with Peter, James, John and Andrew in the company of Jesus, part of me wonders if they aren't at least a little bit hopeful that Jesus will tell them this will all take place long after they have left this world for heaven.

Because, let's face it, who wants to be around to watch the destruction of their world?

But as is His way, Jesus doesn't answer their question. Instead, Jesus continues His dire predictions, painting what at first glance appear to be dark, foreboding pictures of suffering, of sadness, of ruin (including the ruin of Jerusalem), of wars and disasters, and of the suffering of His disciples because of their relationship with Him.

I can't help but wonder if they question their decision to follow Jesus right now. Are they second guessing their choice? Because I am. Being singled out and being put on trial? Being betrayed by family and friends? Being hated, being flogged, maybe even dying? All because of Jesus? I don't know about Peter, James, John and Andrew, but that's not what I was signing up for when I decided to follow Jesus.

In that moment on the shore of the Sea of Galilee when He first showed up and said, "Come, follow me," I certainly didn't foresee doom and gloom and hardship. And that certainly wasn't what I expected when we followed Him here to Jerusalem to celebrate the Passover with Him. Until now, we've watched Him heal, cast out demons, bring the dead back to life, and seen Him turn water into wine. It's been miracle after miracle.

Sure, he's had some run-ins with the Pharisees and exchanged some harsh words. But that's the Pharisees, not the disciples. Where the disciples love and follow Jesus, the Pharisees and other religious leaders despise and condemn Him and seek to turn the crowds against Him. When Jesus is harsh with them, calling them a brood of vipers and hypocrites, that makes sense.

But despite those exchanges, there were still miracles and dinners and celebrations. What happened to the Jesus of miracles? What happened to the Jesus of love and celebration? Where did the Jesus of compassion and hope go? Suddenly He's the Jesus of doom, despair and dire predictions. No, this is definitely not what I signed up for.

But here I sit.

When Jesus finishes speaking, we sit in silence, each with our own thoughts. I cannot help but wonder, what does all of this mean? Why is Jesus telling us this? Is Jesus painting as hopeless a picture for His followers as it appears?

As much as it may seem like it, I don't think so. Because for one thing, with Jesus there is always hope. No matter the path, no matter the circumstances, no matter where we are or what we face, there is hope with Jesus. And the world can definitely use that hope - the hope of healing, the hope of new life, the hope in His presence.

That hope is what I hold on to as we sit here on the Mount of Olives. In fact, I recognize it when I look into the eyes of Jesus and as I gaze around at the faces of the disciples who are here with me. I find Jesus' words in this moment, despite how they frighten and confuse me, draw me closer to Him rather than repel me. The nearer I am to Him, the greater sense of comfort I draw from His presence with me. Because the thing is, even here, even now, He is still the Jesus of hope.

And that, *that* is definitely what I signed up for. No matter the cost. No matter how little I understand sometimes. No matter what.

When the path is dark and seems impassable.

When there is hurt I cannot bear.

When there is despair rather than celebration.

When I long for a miracle but experience only silence.

Even when life is incredibly difficult, there is hope and Jesus is with me. His presence surrounds me and He will never abandon me.

And, yes, that is what I signed up for when He said, "Come. Follow me."

Prayer

Dear Jesus, thank you for the hope and the victory you so freely give to those who follow you. Sometimes life's circumstances and the world's events can create fear, worry and doubt. They can overwhelm me if I focus on them instead of you and your sovereignty. Thank you for your ever-present light and hope as I focus on and follow you.

Additional Scripture for Reflection

Romans 4:17-19

Ephesians 1:15-23

Colossians 1:4-7

Day 26: No Ordinary Man

"So when you see the abomination of desolation—spoken about by Daniel the prophet—standing in the holy place" (let the reader understand), "then those in Judea must flee to the mountains. The one on the roof must not come down to take anything out of his house, and the one in the field must not turn back to get his cloak. Woe to those who are pregnant and to those who are nursing their babies in those days! Pray that your flight may not be in winter or on a Sabbath. For then there will be a great suffering unlike anything that has happened from the beginning of the world until now, or ever will happen. And if those days had not been cut short, no one would be saved. But for the sake of the elect those days will be cut short. Then if anyone says to you, 'Look, here is the Christ!' or 'There he is!' do not believe him. For false messiahs and false prophets will appear and perform great signs and wonders to deceive, if possible, even the elect. Remember, I have told you ahead of time. So then, if someone says to you, 'Look, he is in the wilderness', do not go out, or 'Look, he is in the inner rooms', do not believe him. For just like the lightning comes from the east and flashes to the west, so the coming of the Son of Man will be. Wherever the corpse is, there the vultures will gather.

"Immediately after the suffering of those days, the sun will be darkened, and the moon will not give its light; the stars will fall from heaven, and the powers of heaven will be shaken. Then the sign of the Son of Man will appear in heaven, and all the tribes of the earth will mourn. They will see the Son of Man arriving on the clouds of heaven with power and great glory. And he will send his angels with a loud trumpet blast, and they

will gather his elect from the four winds, from one end of heaven to the other.

"Learn this parable from the fig tree: Whenever its branch becomes tender and puts out its leaves, you know that summer is near. So also you, when you see all these things, know that he is near, right at the door. I tell you the truth, this generation will not pass away until all these things take place. Heaven and earth will pass away, but my words will never pass away." Matthew 24:15-35

This journey with Jesus, this journey to Jerusalem, is beginning to feel like a bit of a steep uphill climb. Maybe even a bit more than a bit of a steep uphill climb. Today is a little like the movie, *Groundhog Day,* scripture wise. Today is more doom and gloom and warnings. Where I am yearning for miracles and intimate meals with my Savior, Jesus is offering tribulation and indefinite darkness and the heavens being shaken, with the stars falling from the sky and all the earth in mourning.

It gives me pause to say the least. No matter how many times He repeats these warnings. Because as we sit here, still on the Mount of Olives, I have asked Him to repeat Himself several times. And, because He is Jesus, He patiently complies.

"You are talking about some specific events," I tell Him. "I get that part."

He nods.

"But I don't get the sense that those things are what you and I are going to talk about," I say.

"No, we're not," He agrees. His dark brown eyes hold my gaze and it feels like He is looking not just in my eyes but in my heart. He smiles and a joy radiates from deep in my heart to each of my cells. I feel like I radiate an energy. As if joy and love are something any passerby can see on me. Shining out from me, shining off my skin.

I watch Him as He reclines against a tree. He has kind eyes and a sense of urgency about His time here. But for now, He focuses on me. He makes me feel like I am the most important thing to Him right now.

That is the thing about Jesus, I think to myself as I continue to look at Him. This must have been what Simon and Andrew and James and John saw in Him the first time they saw Him. This sense that all of His attention was directed at them. Only them.

But it's not just what you feel when He looks at you. It's what you see when you look at Him.

Sitting here now I can see that there is something about Him. Something in Him. It's more than His love, more than His peace. It's an intimacy. An intimate interest in me that I can feel and that I can hear even when He isn't speaking.

Maybe that's why even as He talks about the destruction of the Temple and the ruin of Jerusalem and the tribulations that will come before He does, before He comes again, I am not afraid.

Because He is God. He is not just Jesus, the son of a carpenter. He is not just an ordinary man. He is God.

His journey to this place today started in the stable in Bethlehem.

His journey to this place today started in the Garden of Eden.

His journey to this place today started before time, before space, before anything else existed.

This is His journey because this is His world.

"This is your world," I whisper to Him up here on the Mount of Olives as we look out over Jerusalem.

"It is," He replies.

"All of the beauty, all of the pain, all of the mess. It's all yours."

He nods and His eyes shine with the joy that one sees in the eyes of a new dad. Eyes that reflect hope, and expectation and joy and love. Unconditional love.

Because we are His children. We create beauty, we cause pain, we make messes, we destroy, we build, we love.

We love.

We love because He first loved us. And that is the reason for this journey. That is the miracle really.

I look at this man who is also God and I am filled with awe. An awe that is real. An awe that is powerful. An awe that takes my breath away.

Because I am why He came. I am why He started this journey even before time or the world existed. I am why He will continue this journey even when it takes Him to the cross.

Parts of this journey are difficult for me. Some of His words don't make sense to me. I don't understand everything He does. But I realize that I don't have to understand everything I see and hear. I just need to follow Him. All the way to the cross.

I just need to follow Him. So I do.

Prayer

Dear Jesus, I confess that sometimes your words are challenging to hear and even more difficult to understand. But even so, you invite me to follow you and to sit with you. You invite me to trust you. And as I do, as I sit with you in stillness and silence, you remind me that it is more about our relationship than understanding every word or meaning of Scripture. As I get to know you more, I begin to understand your Word and your message. It all begins with my relationship with you. Thank you for reminding me of that.

Additional Scripture for Reflection

Ephesians 2:8-10

Isaiah 40:28-31

1 John 4:7-12

Day 25: The Time Is Now

"But as for that day and hour no one knows it—not even the angels in heaven—except the Father alone. For just like the days of Noah were, so the coming of the Son of Man will be. For in those days before the flood, people were eating and drinking, marrying and giving in marriage, until the day Noah entered the ark. And they knew nothing until the flood came and took them all away. It will be the same at the coming of the Son of Man. Then there will be two men in the field; one will be taken and one left. There will be two women grinding grain with a mill; one will be taken and one left.

"Therefore stay alert because you do not know on what day your Lord will come. But understand this: If the owner of the house had known at what time of night the thief was coming, he would have been alert and would not have let his house be broken into. Therefore you also must be ready because the Son of Man will come at an hour when you do not expect him.

"Who then is the faithful and wise slave, whom the master has put in charge of his household, to give the other slaves their food at the proper time? Blessed is that slave whom the master finds at work when he comes. I tell you the truth, the master will put him in charge of all his possessions. But if that evil slave should say to himself, 'My master is staying away a long time', and he begins to beat his fellow slaves and to eat and drink with drunkards, then the master of that slave will come on a day when he does not expect him and at an hour he does

not foresee, and will cut him in two, and assign him a place with the hypocrites, where there will be weeping and gnashing of teeth. **Matthew 24:36-51**

I look around at the four disciples — Peter, James, John and Andrew — and I can tell by looking at them they don't want to miss a moment. They want to be ready. Ready for whenever these events come to pass. So they listen without interrupting. They ask no questions. And I marvel at their restraint.

Because I have so many questions, too many questions. Questions I wish Jesus would answer. Because this is important. He is telling us about the ruin of Jerusalem and the impending darkness and the tribulations that will come right before He does.

This is important. And a little frightening. And incredibly overwhelming.

I want to know, where will I be? Will I be ready? Am I prepared?

Does Jesus think I'm ready? Do I?

I think about this. I consider His words.

Is my ark ready or am I too busy eating and drinking and chasing the things of this world?

Am I ready or have I become unaware? So much so that I will be washed away in the flood. Or that the thief will come and will break into my house.

I cannot stop the questions or my fears from forming and I know that Jesus can sense them. I know that He can see them when He looks in my eyes. When He looks at me, I look away, embarrassed for Him to see me naked in my doubt, in my guilt, in my shame. But this is Jesus. And these are the very reasons He sits here right now. To remove doubt. To erase guilt. To eradicate shame.

Jesus, dear Jesus. Here to provide freedom. Come to offer grace.

Jesus, dear, sweet Jesus, Am I ready?

This is the question my heart asks Him. With trepidation my heart implores Him, *Will I be taken? Will I be left?*

What my heart is really asking is, *Please. Please say the words I long to hear. Please.*

Because it's not really about being left behind. Jesus already knows that. It's about whether I've done all I was given to do. It's about whether I've truly loved God with all my heart, with all my mind, with all my soul, with all my strength. It's about whether I've loved my neighbor as myself.

Or have I loved myself too much?

Jesus, dear, sweet Jesus. I want to hear those words, the ones from your Word. I want to hear you say, *Well done, good and faithful servant.*

And as I consider how I live, that is when the doubt, the guilt and the shame build.

But this is Jesus.

He has seen it all. He has seen betrayal and hatred, and suffering that I cannot begin to imagine. He has seen the darkness devour and the goodness recoil. But He has also seen the beauty one person creates push back the very same darkness. And He has heard a lone voice speak love, speak truth, speak life and provide hope.

And as I consider how I live, I implore Him, *Let me be that one person. Let me be that lone voice.*

This journey with Jesus is changing me. It is changing my focus. It is changing what I thought I wanted. It is breaking my heart, refining me with fire and purifying me with His love. When the time comes, I want to be ready. I want to have left nothing behind that was given me to do. I want to have changed the world because Jesus changed me. I want to change the world with Jesus. Because I know this is part of my purpose; it comes because I am His. I am not my own.

Here, on the Mount of Olives, I lean into Jesus. I lay my head on His shoulder and know that I am loved. And that every day I am being made ready as I spend time with Him.

Prayer

Dear Jesus, thank you for your saving grace and for your love that sought me and for the blood that bought my freedom. Thank you for making me a new creation and for inviting me to change the world with you. Thank you that you created good works for me to do and that your Holy Spirit continues to refine me to complete those works.

Additional Scripture for Reflection

Matthew 25:14-30

Ephesians 4:1-8

Colossians 3:1-16

A Day of Reading and Reflection

Scripture for Reflection:

Exodus 20:1-17

God spoke all these words:

"I, the Lord, am your God, who brought you from the land of Egypt, from the house of slavery.

"You shall have no other gods before me.

"You shall not make for yourself a carved image or any likeness of anything that is in heaven above or that is on the earth beneath or that in the waters below. You shall not bow down to them or serve them, for I, the Lord, your God, am a jealous God, responding to the transgression of fathers by dealing with children to the third and fourth generations of those who reject me, and showing covenant faithfulness to a thousand generations of those who love me and keep my commandments.

"You shall not take the name of the Lord your God, in vain, for the Lord will not hold guiltless anyone who takes his name in vain.

"Remember the Sabbath day to set it apart as holy. For six days you may labor and do all your work, but the seventh day is a Sabbath to the Lord your God; on it you shall not do any work, you, or your son or your daughter, or your male servant, or your female servant, or your cattle, or the resident foreigner who is in your gates. For in six days the Lord made the heavens and the earth and

the sea and all that is in them, and he rested on the seventh day; therefore the Lord blessed the Sabbath day and set it apart as holy.

"Honor your father and your mother, that you may live a long time in the land the Lord your God is giving to you.

"You shall not murder.

"You shall not commit adultery.

"You shall not steal.

"You shall not give false testimony against your neighbor.

"You shall not covet your neighbor's house. You shall not covet your neighbor's wife, nor his male servant, nor his female servant, nor his ox, nor his donkey, nor anything that belongs to your neighbor."

Psalm 19 For the music director, a psalm of David

The heavens declare the glory of God;

the sky displays this handiwork.

Day after day it speaks out;

night after night it reveals his greatness.

There is no actual speech or word,

nor is its voice literally heard.

Yet its voice echoes throughout the earth;

its words carry to the distant horizon.

In the sky he has pitched a tent for the sun.

Like a bridegroom it emerges from its chamber;

like a strong man it enjoys running its course.

It emerges from the distant horizon,

and goes from one end of the sky to the other;

nothing can escape its heat.

The law of the LORD is perfect

and preserves one's life.

The rules set down by the Lord are reliable

and impart wisdom to the inexperienced.

The LORD's precepts are fair

and make one joyful.

The LORD's commands are pure,

and give insight for life.

The commands to fear the Lord are right

and endure forever.

The judgments given by the Lord are trustworthy,

and absolutely just.

They are of greater value than gold,

than even a great amount of pure gold;

they bring greater delight than honey,

than even the sweetest honey from a honeycomb.

Yes, your servant finds moral guidance there;

those who obey them receive a rich reward.

Who can know all his errors?

Please do not punish me for sins I am unaware of.

Moreover, keep me from committing flagrant sins;

do not allow such sins to control me.

Then I will be blameless

and innocent of blatant rebellion.

May my words and my thoughts

be acceptable in your sight,

O LORD, my sheltering rock and my redeemer.

1 Corinthians 1:18-25

*For the message of the cross is foolishness to those who are perishing, but to us who are being saved it is the power of God. For it is written, "**I will destroy the wisdom of the wise, and I will thwart the cleverness of the intelligent**." Where is the wise man? Where is the expert in the Mosaic law? Where is the debater of this age? Has God not made the wisdom of the world foolish? For since in the wisdom of God the world by its wisdom did not know God, God was pleased to save those who believe by the foolishness of preaching. For Jews demand miraculous signs and Greeks ask for wisdom, but we preach about a crucified Christ, a stumbling block to Jews and foolishness to Gentiles. But to those who are called, both Jews and Greeks, Christ is the power of God and the* *wisdom of God. For the foolishness of God is wiser than human wisdom, and the weakness of God is stronger than human strength.*

John 2:13-22

Now the Jewish Feast of Passover was near, so Jesus went up to Jerusalem.

*He found in the temple courts those who were selling oxen and sheep and doves, and the money changers sitting at tables. So he made a whip of cords and drove them all out of the temple courts, with the sheep and the oxen. He scattered the coins of the money changers, and overturned their tables. To those who sold the doves he said, "Take these things away from here! Do not make my Father's house a marketplace!" His disciples remembered that it was written, "**Zeal for your house will devour me**."*

So then the Jewish leaders responded, "What sign can you show us, since you are doing these things?" Jesus replied, "Destroy this temple and in three days I will raise it up again." Then the Jewish leaders said to him, "this temple has been under construction for 46 years, and you are going to raise it up in three days?" But Jesus was speaking about the temple of his body. So after he was raised from the dead, his disciples remembered that he had said this, and they believed the scripture and the saying that Jesus had spoken.

Day 24: His Love Trumps My Fear

*"At that time the kingdom of heaven will be like 10 virgins who took their lamps and went out to meet the bridegroom. Five of the virgins were foolish and five were wise. When the foolish ones took their lamps, they did not take extra olive oil with them. But the wise ones took flasks of olive oil with their lamps. When the bridegroom was delayed a long time, they all became drowsy and fell asleep. But at midnight there was a shout, 'Look, the bridegroom is here! Come out to meet him.' Then all the virgins woke up and trimmed their lamps. The foolish ones said to the wise, 'Give us some of your oil because our lamps are going out.' 'No,' they replied. 'There won't be enough for you and for us. Go instead to those who sell oil and buy some for yourselves.' But while they had gone to buy it, the bridegroom arrived, and those who were ready went inside with him to the wedding banquet. Then the door was shut. Later, the other virgins came too, saying, 'Lord, lord! Let us in!' But he replied, "I tell you the truth, I do not know you!' Therefore stay alert because you do not know the day or the hour." **Matthew 25:1-13**

We continue to sit atop the Mount of Olives as Jesus once more impresses upon us our need to be ready, to be wise; not just to hear, but to heed His instructions. Heed His warning. I find myself marveling at His words. A shiver runs through me and I reach out for His hand, gripping it tightly in mine. If I am holding too tightly, He does not say. Nor does He withdraw His hand from mine. Today's illustration unsettles me more than the previous ones.

I believe He senses my need for Him. I believe He senses my need for His reassurance.

I look in His eyes and they tell me it's okay to need His assurance. It's okay to feel afraid. It's okay.

It doesn't feel okay, I tell Him.

I know, He replies softly. *I'm sorry for that.*

A tear spills from my eye and slides down my cheek and His rough carpenter hand reaches out and gently wipes it away. I find comfort in knowing that Jesus knows my heart. That He can read what I hold there.

These are the hardest words I've heard so far on this journey, I say.

He nods and wraps my hand in both of His, a comfort beyond words right now. He waits. He doesn't distract or offer me empty words. Instead He lets me wander through my own heavy words. Words heavy with questions. Words heavy with uncertainty. Words that instill fear, not hope. I long for hope. In fact I hunger for it right now.

Only you can know a person's heart, I begin.

Yes, He agrees.

That has always been the hard part, you know?

Jesus nods; His eyes are filled with love and compassion.

Sheepishly, I admit to Him, *I've never really understood this story. I've read it plenty of times, but I've never really looked at what it's saying.*

Jesus smiles. There is no judgment for this confession. *But today you are,* He says.

I nod slowly, closing my eyes and considering this most recent parable, especially the real implications it holds for my life.

Ten virgins go out to await the bridegroom and five go into the marriage celebration and five are left outside after the door closes. The door won't open again. They will stay in the dark. They will stay apart from the bridegroom. I do not worry that I will be one of the ones outside the closed door. That is not what causes me to fret today, sitting beside my Savior listening to this story. My concern is for people I love. For those I call friend. For those whose blood runs through my veins.

The ten virgins all appear the same. They all take up their lamps. They all go out to look for the bridegroom, to await his arrival. They all stay up until the wait becomes long and sleep takes them over. The only difference is that five virgins are called wise because they bring extra oil.

The other five? They are called foolish. They bring only the lamp but no additional oil.

When the wait stretches late into the dark of the night, the lamps begin to burn low. And when the bridegroom's procession finally arrives, only the five who have enough oil can find their way to the procession. Only they find their way to the entrance into the marriage celebration.

Hearing the story of the bridegroom and taking up your lamp to go out and seek Him is not enough. Following faithful followers will only get you so far; it won't get you into the party. But that's not the point. That's not what I am supposed to focus on right now.

Jesus looks at me expectantly at this point. Because He knows. He, too, knows that this isn't about them or their actions. This is about me.

This is about what I can do, isn't it? I ask.

I know the answer, but I want Him to confirm what I am learning sitting here with Him.

It is, He says.

I ask myself, *If God today answered every prayer I prayed today or yesterday or last week, would there be anybody new in the Kingdom of God tomorrow?*

Tears spill steadily from my eyes now. Because if I answer this question honestly, if I answer Jesus' question that underlies the conversation this parable has inspired between us, my only answer is, *No.* No, there would not be anybody new in the Kingdom of God tomorrow. Or Yesterday. Or last week.

Rather there likely would be those left standing outside the door, still in the darkness. Still seeking, carrying lamps in need of oil.

Each of us is responsible for choosing a relationship with Jesus. We can't choose that for anyone but ourselves. Even so, we can affect others, influencing them by how we live and reflecting the face of God in this world.

And each of us in a relationship with Jesus is also responsible for sharing the Good News. For praying for those who don't know Him. For shining a Light in the darkness of the world. For shining a Light in the darkness of the lives of those around us. Family. Friends. Neighbors. Strangers. Like that person you passed on the street with tears in her eyes, that person behind the counter who is busy and frazzled and in need of a kind word.

Is there really anything more important we can do than to pray for people to come to know Jesus?

Is there really anything more pressing than to introduce someone to the Savior?

It scares me, I whisper, looking at the dirt instead of at Jesus.

He pulls me close, still holding my hand in His roughened Creator hands and I take a deep, trembling breath. In the silence on this hill I hear truth in His very breath. I hear truth in my Spirit.

I tremble at the truth.

Because I know that His love trumps the enemy's lie of fear.

Because I know that this is why I am on this journey.

Because I know that I am here for such a time as this.

And His love trumps my fear. Every time.

Prayer

Dear Jesus, I confess that sometimes I let my fear keep me from sharing the Good News of your love and grace and forgiveness. I am sorry for the opportunities I have missed before today and I ask you today to guide me to live out your Truth in my life and in the world. Help me, Jesus, to live a life worthy of your sacrifice and your Good News. Help me to live boldly and fearlessly and to proclaim your name and bring you glory in my words and my deeds.

Additional Scripture for Reflection

Philippians 1:12-20

Revelation 21:3-8

1 John 4:16-19

Day 23: Time for a Little Recklessness

"For it is like a man going on a journey, who summoned his slaves and entrusted his property to them. To one he gave five talents, to another two, and to another one, each according to his ability. Then he went on his journey. The one who had received five talents went off right away and put his money to work and gained five more. In the same way, the one who had two gained two more. But the one who had received one talent went out and dug a hole in the ground and hid his master's money in it. After a long time, the master of those slaves came and settled his accounts with them. The one who had received the five talents came and brought five more, saying, 'Sir, you entrusted me with five talents. See, I have gained five more.' His master answered, 'Well done, good and faithful slave! You have been faithful in a few things. I will put you in charge of many things. Enter into the joy of your master.' The one with the two talents also came and said, 'Sir, you entrusted two talents to me. See, I have gained two more.' His master answered, 'Well done, good and faithful slave! You have been faithful with a few things. I will put you in charge of many things. Enter into the joy of your master.' Then the one who had received the one talent came and said, 'Sir, I knew that you were a hard man, harvesting where you did not sow, and gathering where you did not scatter seed, so I was afraid, and I went and hid your talent in the ground. See, you

have what is yours.' But his master answered, 'Evil and lazy slave! So you knew that I harvest where I didn't sow and gather where I didn't scatter? Then you should have deposited my money with the bankers, and on my return I would have received my money back with interest! Therefore take the talent from him and give it to the one who has 10. For the one who has will be given more, and he will have more than enough. But the one who does not have, even what he has will be taken from him. And throw that worthless slave into the outer darkness, where there will be weeping gnashing of teeth.'" **Matthew 25:14-30**

Today I am restless. We have been sitting up here on the Mount of Olives for several days and I am ready to move on. I am ready for Jesus to move on. To move on to a new place. To move on to a new topic. I pace in the shade of a tree and stare out over the busy bustling streets of Jerusalem below.

Of course, this parable is the one, the one that includes the words I yearn to hear: "Well done, good and faithful servant." That is the part I know best, but I am equally familiar with the words that describe the Master's reward: "You have been faithful over a little; I will set you over much."

I have used these words to motivate myself past fear in the past, especially when I am using my gifts. The gifts I believe were given to me by God. I have sought to honor the Creator with my gifts and my talents in the smallest ways so that He will provide me greater opportunities. Because I truly believe that these gifts that were given me are best used in service to Jesus.

To bring Him glory. To bring Him honor. To point people to Him.

This has not always been easy for me. Especially as one who is drawn to the spotlight, who wants to be the center of attention, who inserts herself into the stories of others without much hesitation or invites others into her story without thinking twice.

But these are not the ideas I contemplate today. Today I am struck by the other words the Master in the parable says. Today, as I stand here in the heat of the Jerusalem sun, I consider the parable's promise: "Enter into the joy of your Master."

Certainly, this beats the alternative. This beats being cast into the outer darkness. This beats being thrown out into the place where there is only weeping and gnashing of teeth. Because isn't there enough of that right here? Don't we see too much of that, don't we do too much of that right now, in the here and now?

Don't I *do* that too much in the here and now? Too much fretting. Too much complaining. Too much wailing and gnashing my teeth. Too much me, me, me. Too much *what's in it for me?* Too much *what about me?* Too much *what will I gain if I do this or that?*

I look over at Jesus sitting among His inner circle of disciples - Peter, James, John, Andrew. In between these parables and warnings, mixed in among all this serious conversation, Jesus and His disciples talk and laugh. Their joy fills the stifling sweltering air and their easy comfortable manner reveals the strong, intimate friendship these men share.

Despite moments of wanting to know which of them is Jesus' favorite, these men are the epitome of selflessness and service. Walking with the Savior through His ministry, witnessing miracles, performing miracles of their own. And always, always, they put the focus on Jesus. They turn their focus on Jesus. These disciples have indeed entered into the joy of their Master. They will suffer greatly and soon. Jesus has warned them of that. But right now, even as they discuss the serious events that are coming, they are wrapped in the joy of the Savior.

I come back to the idea of the talents. The way the first and second servants departed immediately and with reckless abandon. How they doubled what they received originally. The way they acted because of their relationship to the Master as well as with the Master. How they acted because they were entrusted with something important, something valuable, and their actions showed how much they valued what they had been given and what they had been asked to do.

The third servant, on the other hand, acted from a place of fear and doubt. He acted based on assumptions of cruelty and harshness. His actions do not demonstrate any sense of being entrusted with anything, but being burdened with something. Something for which he does not want to be responsible. And his actions clearly do not demonstrate a relationship with the Master.

The disciples' laughter ripples in waves, reaching me where I stand. Peter lays back on the ground looking up at the sky, the easy smile lingering on his face. He is the picture of contentment. Of joy. He would easily be the first servant. Impetuous Peter. I wander back over to the group and flop down in between Jesus and Peter. I have identified with Peter for a good portion of my life. The first to jump up and proclaim Jesus and shout out my love for Him and the first to deny Him and betray Him. But I have learned the art of joy and contentment from watching Peter with Jesus.

I have learned how to take what has been entrusted to me and share it with reckless abandon. To use it to bring glory to Jesus. To use it to point others to Jesus. I have learned how to let Jesus' love for me trump the lie of fear. I have learned how to sit beside Jesus, like now, knowing that because I love Him I may know suffering or strife or heartbreak but that even so I have entered into his joy. No more will I cast myself into the darkness alone or will I feel abandoned in the place of weeping and gnashing of teeth. I am wrapped in the joy, the grace, the love, the hope of Jesus.

I have entered into the joy of my Master. I am living my life for Him. I am sharing his love and his hope through the gifts, the talents, with which He entrusted me. And that makes life worth living. That makes all the difference. In the here and now and in the Kingdom of God.

If you are not willing to live your life for something greater than yourself, well, then life does not hold the real value that God so freely gives us in it and in Him.

Prayer

Dear Jesus, thank you for difficult words and lessons that hold such value and remind me of the greater Story you are weaving in my life and in the world. Thank you for the gifts, the talents, you have entrusted to me. I pray that when I hold them too tightly, when I am afraid to use them, you Spirit will pierce me with this beautiful reminder and that I will remember this moment and the joy and contentment that come from serving you.

Additional Scripture for Reflection

Psalm 98

Philippians 2:12-16

Colossians 3:23-25

Day 22: What's It Going to Be?

"When the Son of Man comes in his glory and all the angels with him, then he will sit on his glorious throne. All the nations will be assembled before him, and he will separate the sheep on his right and the goats on his left. Then the king will say to those on his right, 'Come, you who are blessed by my Father, inherit the kingdom prepared for you from the foundation of the world. Then the righteous will answer him, 'Lord, when did we see you hungry and feed you, or thirsty and give you something to drink? When did we see you a stranger and invite you in, or naked and clothe you? When did we see you sick or in prison and visit you?' And the king will answer them, 'I tell you the truth, just you did it for one of the least of these brother or sisters of mine, you did it for me.'

"Then he will say to hose on his left, 'Depart from me, you accursed, into the eternal fire that has been prepared for the devil and his angels! For I was hungry and you gave me nothing to eat, I was thirsty and you gave me nothing to drink. I was a stranger and you did not receive me as a guest, naked and you did not clothe me sick and in prison and you did not visit me.' Then they too will answer, 'Lord, when did we see you hungry or thirsty or a stronger or naked or sick or in prison, and did not give you whatever you needed?' Then he will answer them, 'I tell you the truth, just as you did not do it for one of the least of these, you did not do it for me.' And these

*will depart into eternal punishment, but the righteous into eternal life." **Matthew 25:31-46***

When I started out on this journey with Jesus to Jerusalem three weeks ago, I had no idea where it would lead. I knew that we would travel some difficult terrain. And I knew that eventually I would end up at the foot of the cross. But the moments in between? The moments leading to the cross? I really didn't know what to expect.

And, to be honest, this not knowing, it's become more of a challenge recently. And it's made me want to cheat. It's made me want to read ahead in the 40+ days of scriptures that I get one day at a time so that I can cherry pick the ones that will make this journey easier. Easier to make. Easier to write about.

Because it's become more about writing about the journey, not about being on the journey.

Because it's become about building an audience, not about building my relationship.

Because it's become about me, not about Jesus. About my blog, about my writing, about my insights.

Except that's not what I set out to do three weeks ago.

But if there's one thing I've learned in my {somewhat inconsistent} walk with Jesus in my life, it's that the journey with Jesus can take on a direction I never intended if I am not intentional.

If I am not intentional.

Of course even if I am not intentional, the journey can still take a turn for the good, for *my* good. But most of the time, when I am not intentional, the journey will take a turn for the not-so-good, like now. When it becomes more about what I can get from Jesus rather than what I can give to Him. When it becomes more about what Jesus is going to do for me rather than what I am going to do for Him. When it becomes more about Jesus as a genie granting my wishes or about Jesus as an accessory rather than about Jesus as the Creator of the universe who wants a personal relationship with me or about Jesus as the reason for my being. About Jesus as the reason for my next breath.

This morning, when I rejoined Jesus and His disciples on the Mount of Olives, I felt deeply convicted. I felt like one of the goats in Jesus' parable, set apart, but not in a good way. In reality, I am not a goat. I have a relationship with Jesus. I daily acknowledge my need for Him even as I daily return to Him more times than I can count. Even as I daily forget whose I am.

But even so, I recognize that even as one of the Shepherd's sheep, I have wandered off with the goats. I have lost sight of my Shepherd, replacing Him with my need for the world's recognition, the world's applause, the world's approval. I have allowed the world to push Jesus aside.

And so I pause. I breathe. I wait. And then I cry out. I cry out to Him whom my heart loves. I cry out to I AM.

Because I am a sheep lost along the path. Because I am a sheep in need of her Shepherd. Because I am a woman in need of her Savior's second chance {for the 1,273rd time}. A woman in need of her Savior's presence on this journey. This daily journey through life.

This daily journey that is also a journey to draw near to Jesus. A journey to know the Shepherd, my Savior, my Jesus more than I do today. More than I do right now. And so I sit down near the disciples. Near Jesus. But apart from them. At least a little bit.

But Jesus, Jesus will have none of this separation. He will have none of my shame. He moves over to where I am and without any effort by me, I am back in the fold. I am counted as one of His sheep.

I am counted as one of His disciples.

I am counted as one of His own. *As one of His own.*

And I wonder at how easy it is to get off track with Jesus. How easily I lose my way and let the world crowd Him out, push Him out. How easily I worry about the things of this world despite what I know. Despite who I know. I do not know where this journey leads tomorrow. But I know with whom I go. I know Him whom my heart loves. And He knows me. He knows me.

{And He loves me anyway.}

Prayer

Dear Jesus, Thank you that you are a God of second, third and 1,232nd chances. Thank you for being the Good Shepherd who leaves behind the 99 in order to find the one who has gone astray, like me. Me, the one who has gotten distracted by the world and the things it offers. I am thankful for your Spirit that guides me back to the path and reminds me of the joy that comes in you.

Additional Scripture for Reflection

Luke 12:22-31

Luke 15:1-7

Matthew 6:19-27

Day 21: Living My Life with Purpose

Now some Greeks were among those who had gone up to worship at the feast. So these approached Philip, who was from Bethsaida in Galilee, and requested, "sir we would like to see Jesus." Philip went and told Andrew, and the both went and told Jesus. Jesus replied, "The time has come for the Son of Man to be glorified. I tell you the solemn truth, unless a kernel of wheat falls into the ground and dies, it remains by itself alone. But if it dies, it produces much grain. The one who loves his life destroys it, and the one who hates his life in this world guards it for eternal life. If anyone wants to serve me, he must follow me, and where I am, my servant will be too. If anyone serves me, the Father will honor him.

"Now my should is greatly distressed. And what should I say? 'Father, deliver me from this hour'? No, but for this very reason I have come to this hour. Father, glorify your name." Then a voice came from heaven, "I have glorified it, and I will glorify it again." The crowd that stood there and heard the voice said that it had thundered. Others said that an angel had spoken to him. Jesus said, "This voice has not come for my benefit but for yours. Now is the judgment of this world; now the ruler of this world will be driven out. And I, when I am lifted up from the earth, will draw all the people to myself." (Now he said this to indicate clearly what kind of death he was going to die.)

Then the crowd responded, "We have heard from the law that the Christ will remain forever. How can you say, 'The Son of Man must be lifted up'? Who is this Son of Man?" Jesus replied, "The light is with you for a little while longer. Walk while you have the light, so that the darkness may not overtake you. The one who walks in the darkness does not know where he is going. While you have the light, believe in the light, so that you may become sons of light." When Jesus had said these things, he went away and hid himself from them.

Although Jesus had performed so many miraculous signs before them, they still refused to believe in him, so that the word of the prophet Isaiah would be fulfilled. He said, **"Lord, who has believed our message, and to whom has the arm of the Lord been revealed?"** For this reason they could not believe, because again Isaiah said,

> **"He has blinded their eyes**
>
> **and hardened their heart,**
>
> **so that they would not see with their eyes**
>
> **and understand with their heart,**
>
> **and turn to me, and I would heal them."**

Isaiah said these things because he saw Christ's glory, and spoke about him.

Nevertheless, even among the rulers many believed in him, but because of the Pharisees they would not confess Jesus to be the Christ, so that they would not be put out of the synagogue. For they loved praise from men more than praise from God.

*But Jesus shouted out, "The one who believes in me does not believe in me, but in the one who sent me, and the one who sees me sees the one who sent me. I have come as a light into the world, so that everyone who believes in me should not remain in darkness. If anyone hears my words and does not obey them, I do not judge him. For I have not come to judge the world, but to save the world. The one who rejects me and does not accept my words has a judge; the word I have spoken will judge him at the last day. For I have not spoken from my own authority, but the Father himself who sent me has commanded me what I should say and what I should speak. And I know that his commandment is eternal life. Thus the things I say, I say just as the Father has told me." **John 12:20-50***

Today finds Jesus on the move again and back among the crowds, being sought after, being questioned. Being doubted.

Many seem to be seeking, to be looking for answers. They have seen Him perform countless miracles. They have seen Him heal lepers and the lame. They have seen Him raise Lazarus from the dead. They want to believe. But He does not quite fit the picture they have of the Messiah, what they have learned about the Christ.

They don't believe in Him. Even so, they cannot stop following Him. He remains compelling, but the world remains more so. And so they are blind to who He is.

Mixed into this crowd are many religious leaders who do believe in Him. But they won't admit it. At least not yet. Because it's still too dangerous, too dangerous to their rank among men, too dangerous to their reputation in the community, and too dangerous to their standing in the synagogue. Even so, they stay close. They follow Him. They listen to Him. They seek His wisdom and long to know Him.

But there are some new faces, too. Outsiders. Curious onlookers who want to meet Him, who want a chance to talk to Him. Even so, they approach His disciples, not Him. We don't know if they meet Him and talk to Him or not. If they had approached Him directly, I'm confident they would have had as much time to talk with Him as they wanted because He has a track record for giving those who sought it His attention.

And in the middle of it all, there is Jesus. Jesus who is God. Jesus who is man.

Jesus.

Jesus who knows what is coming. Jesus who comes to save and not to judge. Jesus who comes to suffer.

Jesus.

Jesus who will willingly suffer in order to save. And though His human soul is deeply troubled, His existence as the Son of God pushes Him forward.

By His Light He casts out darkness. By His obedience He brings glory to the Father. By His sacrifice He defeats the ruler of this world.

But it is no easy sacrifice.

Already I see the struggle He faces. His words give me a glimpse of His humanity. He is deeply troubled. Would that He could be saved from the cross, from the suffering.

But then how would we fare?

Unless a grain of wheat falls. Unless the seed dies. Unless.

Unless the Savior, this Jesus, my Jesus is lifted up, nailed to the cross, the world remains hopeless. The crowds continue to yearn, to seek, to doubt. You and I stumble through darkness, through sadness, at the whim of the ruler of this world.

Only when He is lifted up will all who seek Him, who need Him, who believe in Him be gathered to Him.

Only when He is lifted up will the enemy be defeated and the darkness pushed back.

Only when He is lifted up will we know God again, the way God intended for us to know Him: *intimately*.

He has walked among us. He has laughed with us. He has cried with us. He has healed us. He has performed miracles in front of us.

Even so, His purpose is beyond us.

It is beyond here. It is beyond these few moments.

His purpose is eternal. It is not about a single moment in the middle of a crowd that is seeking, doubting, wanting, wondering, wishing, needing, longing.

It is about Him. It is about Jesus.

It's about approaching Him directly. It's about following Him without fear. It's about finding truth and knowing God.

It's about life.

Abundant life and eternal life.

It's about life lived in grace. About life lived in hope. About life lived in victory.

It's about a life, my life, lived with purpose. On purpose.

Because He lived out His purpose. And I was part of His purpose.

Prayer

Dear Jesus, how amazing it is to consider what you did for me, even before I knew you. To see you on this journey is to see your purpose as well as your love. To know that you could have said, *No*, but you didn't. To be forgiven by such an extravagant act of love and sacrifice. Thank you, Jesus, for abundant life and for grace freely given and for hope that never dies. Thank you for the opportunity to live in victory and on purpose every day.

Additional Scripture for Reflection

John 10: 1-13

1 Corinthians 15:50-58

2 Corinthians 5:18-21

Day 20: A Dream Worth the Wait

Now on the first day of the feast of Unleavened Bread, when the Passover lamb is sacrificed, Jesus' disciples said to him, "Where do you want us to prepare for you to eat the Passover?" He sent two of his disciples and told them, "Go into the city, and a man carrying a jar of water will meet you. Follow him. Wherever he enters, tell the owner of the house, 'The Teacher says, "Where is my guest room where I may eat the Passover with my disciples?"' He will show you a large room upstairs, furnished and ready. Make preparations for us there." So the disciples left, went into the city, and found things just as he had told them, and they prepared the Passover.

Then, when it was evening, he came to the house with the twelve. While they were at the table eating, Jesus said, "I tell you the truth, one of you eating with me will betray me." They were distressed, and one by one said to him, "Surely not I?" He said to them, "It is one of the twelve, one who dips his hand with me into the bowl. For the Son of Man will go as it is written about him, but woe to that man by whom the Son of Man is betrayed! It would be better for him if he had never been born."

While they were eating, he took bread, and after giving thanks he broke it, gave it to them, and said, "Take it. This is my body." And after taking the cup and giving thanks, he gave it to them, and they all drank from it. He said to them, "This is my blood, the blood of the covenant, that is poured out for many. I tell you the truth, I will no longer drink of the fruit of the vine until that day when I drink it new in the kingdom of God." After singing a hymn, they went out to the Mount of Olives. **Mark 14:12-26**

I sit, knees drawn up and hugged close to my chest, my chin resting on my knees, soaking in the scene. We are in a large upper room. Jesus and His disciples have gathered for an intimate meal, the Passover meal. Everything is exactly the way Jesus predicted: the man carrying a jar of water; a gracious, generous homeowner; an upper room furnished, prepared, ready.

But who is the Master of this house? Is he a relative of Jesus? Otherwise, why was he expecting Jesus? What prompted him to prepare, to furnish a guest room for Jesus and His disciples? I wonder if maybe he had a dream, a vision, a God-ordained vision of just this moment.

Did he wake up one day, maybe years ago, having dreamt the night before about two men who would come to him, come to his house, this house, seeking a place to prepare a Passover meal with friends? And did his dream include Jesus? The Jesus who sits here now. Jesus the Christ. Jesus the Messiah. Jesus the Passover Lamb. I don't know, but how could he not have had some God-given vision? We know Jesus clearly knew about this man, that he had a servant who would fetch water, that he had an upper room, and that he had a generous spirit. To me, if Jesus knew this, it isn't too great a leap to think that God has been preparing this man, too. Laid this dream, this vision, on his heart years ago.

Can you imagine it?

He knew they would come, but not when.

He waited every day leading up to Passover, looking, hoping, anticipating.

He prepared this upper room each Passover, waiting for these men who now fill this room, only to undo it all when they didn't show up.

What did he think when the men did not come?

What did he think as the years went by and still his dream remained only a dream? Only a vision. A vision that he believed in his heart, in his soul, to be from God. One that he held onto even though there was no reason to other than what he believed. How easy it would have been to give up. But apparently he didn't and at last, they are here.

Can you imagine it?

Can you imagine what today must have been like for him? Can you imagine what it's like to have Jesus sitting in this room with His disciples?

For such a time as this.

All these years waiting and being ready and today, finally today, the dream he refused to give up believing is unfolding before him. Here are the two men for whom he has been waiting. Here are the two men who ask him, 'The Teacher says, 'Where is my guest room, where I may eat the Passover with my disciples?''

For such a time as this.

Where was he when they finally showed up? What was he doing when they finally arrived? Was he upstairs, finishing up the final preparations on this room? Or was he working somewhere out back when he heard them come in, looking for him, calling out to him.

For such a time as this.

And his faithfulness has been rewarded. Jesus has come to this house. Jesus has come to *his* house. Jesus sits in the upper room that this man prepared and made ready. Jesus is here.

What an incredible sense of elation and emotion this man must have. Not only today, but at the time he received his dream. Knowing that he would play a role in this moment. Knowing that he was waiting for such a time as this.

Certainly such a dream can only come from God. Certainly such a dream can only be done *with* God.

And I wonder. Do I have a dream like that? Has God given me a vision for something that brings me joy and anticipation and the strength to see it through? Even if it means that I have to wait? And then wait some more? Even if it means that I get ready for the moment, but the moment is not yet?

Do I have a dream like that?

Because I know I want one. I want a dream so big that it will take God to make it happen. I want a dream that will have Jesus showing up and being there. I want a dream that has Jesus in the midst of my efforts, that has Jesus as the reason for my efforts, that has Jesus expecting what I have been given to do.

I want a dream that has Jesus sending people to me because He knows that I will be ready.

Like this man was ready.

For such a time as this.

I dabble in dreaming, but I am not truly *daring* to dream, not a big, faith-filled, *faithful-to-Jesus* dream. In fact, too often recently, I'm afraid to dream. I haven't claimed my God-ordained vision. But I think it's time. I think I *need* to. So I am going to look at this life I've been given, take it up in my hands, and offer it to God. I want to see what He will do with it.

For my part, I will get up each day looking, hoping, and anticipating - preparing for what I know and believing in what I do. And the only way that can happen is if God gives me His vision. If I let God dream for me. If I surrender my control to His.

If I am ready for such a time as this.

And I am.

Prayer

Dear Jesus, thank you for this powerful picture of faith. For years as I've read this passage I wondered about Judas' role and how the disciples didn't realize he was the one to whom you referred. But this time, you have shown me something new and for that I am incredibly grateful. And I look to you and to the days to come with great anticipation and I wait to see what you will do when I offer all of me to all of you. I look forward to uncovering the desires of my heart that you have placed there, Lord.

Additional Scripture for Reflection

Esther 4:13-17

Jeremiah 29:11-14

Genesis 69-22

Day 19: Jesus: A Portrait of Love

Just before the Passover feast, Jesus knew that his time had come to depart from this world to the Father. Having loved his own who were in the world, he now loved them to the very end. The evening meal was in progress, and the devil had already put into the heart of Judas Iscariot, Simon's son, that he should betray Jesus. Because Jesus knew that the Father had handed all things over to him, and that he had come from God and was going back to God, he got up from the meal, removed his outer clothes, took a towel and tied it around himself. He poured water into the washbasin and began to wash the disciples' feet and to dry them with the towel he had wrapped around himself.

Then he came to Simon Peter. Peter said to him, "Lord, are you going to wash my feet?" Jesus replied, "You do not understand what I am doing now, but you will understand after these things." Peter said to him, "You will never wash my feet!" Jesus replied, "If I do not wash you, you have no share with me." Simon Peter said to him, "Lord, wash not only my feet, but also my hands and my head!" Jesus replied, "The one who has bathed needs only to wash his feet, but is completely clean. And you disciples are clean, but not every one of you." (For Jesus knew the one who was going to betray him. For this reason he said, "Not every one of you is clean.")

So when Jesus had washed their feet and put his outer clothing back on, he took his place at the table again and said to them, "Do you understand what I have done for you? You call me 'Teacher' and 'Lord,' and do so correctly, for that is what I am. If I then, your Lord and Teacher, have washed your feet, you too ought to wash one another's feet. For I have given you an example – you should do just as I have done for you. I tell you the solemn truth, the slave is not greater than his master, nor is the one who is sent as a messenger greater than the one who sent him. If you understand these things, you will be blessed if you do them. **John 13:1-17**

This meal is not about the food. It's not about eating together, not about sharing a meal together. This is about something deeply intimate. Something timeless. Something to be treasured. At this meal, Jesus offers an incredibly beautiful portrait of love. Intimate, unconditional, amazing love. Even as His life is drawing to its end here on earth, Jesus remains focused on others, on His disciples. Even as Jesus prepares to bear the burdens of the world, He bares His heart, His soul, even His human body, to His disciples. As He pours out the water into the basin, He pours out His love in each and every action, in every stroke used to wash His disciples' feet.

Seeing Jesus like this, so vulnerable, so humble, causes me to catch my breath. Is this really God? Kneeling before these men, wearing only a tunic with a towel wrapped around His waist, serving them in the most lowly of ways by washing their feet. Is this what God is like?

This scene before me is both beautiful and disturbing. Disturbing because this Jesus who is God has made himself even lower than man. He has made himself a slave, performing a menial task that takes on an incredible intimacy and beauty because it is done by the Lord.

If it were Peter, impetuous Peter, it would seem a normal thing because he loves to step out, to jump in and to do things others might not.

If it were Judas Iscariot, it would be shocking and surreal because of who he is in his heart and what he is about to do.

But it is Jesus. And so it is intimate. Beautiful. Humbling.

So incredibly humbling, and even a little bit painful to behold, especially when He comes to Judas. The one who will betray Him. The one whose heart is not clean even if his feet are.

Jesus knows Judas' heart. He knows what Judas is going to do. He knew it when He called him to be one of His disciples. He knew it when they shared the Passover meal together. He knew it when they broke bread together and ate of the body and drank of the blood. And He knows now. He knows that Judas will betray Him. He knows that Judas will be the one to bring His mission to its close. Even so, He washes Judas' feet. With the same love, with the same grace, with the same humility, Jesus kneels before Judas and washes the grime of the city from his feet. He scrubs the sand of the miles away. With gentleness, He dries his betrayer's feet. He looks Judas in the eyes and Judas knows He knows.

What kind of love is this?

What kind of God is this?

Is this what God is like?

This is amazing love. This is amazing grace. This is who God is.

This is what love is meant to look like.

And I find myself asking, *Do I love like this?*

Because this is what love is supposed to look like. Jesus says so. I cannot escape His words. I cannot escape His example. I cannot ignore the fact that He washed all of the disciples' feet. He makes no exception for Judas even though He knows the evil that has overtaken Judas' heart.

What excuse have I for not doing likewise? Jesus knew Judas' heart, knew his betrayal, and yet He served him. I have no excuse. I have no excuse to withhold love, to withhold grace, to withhold forgiveness, to withhold helping or serving others. I have no excuse for I know not the heart of any man.

Do I love like this?

If I am honest, I do not. Not nearly as often as I ought. Not if doing so will make me unpopular. Not if doing so will pull me out of my comfort zone. Not if doing so will make me look too "Christian." Because if I am honest, I have looked past a homeless man rather than meet his eyes or offer him my kindness. Because if I am honest, I have not spoken up when words could have made a difference in someone's life. Because if I am honest, I have stood on the sidelines, or worse, stood in the middle of conflicts because I didn't want to hurt anyone else's feelings.

Do I love like this man who is also God?

Not often enough. At least not yet.

But I want to.

I want to focus on others the way Jesus focused on others. I want to be a portrait of intimate, unconditional, amazing love. I want to be vulnerable. I want to be humble. I want to bare my heart and my soul for others to see plainly. I want to bear others' burdens willingly. I want to wash the feet of those who might hurt me or betray me.

I want to love like that. Even if it scares me.

Especially if it scares me.

Prayer

Dear Jesus, thank you for this beautiful example, this beautiful portrait of love and grace and service. Forgive me, Lord, for my pridefulness that keeps me from being an imitator of your love and grace. And thank you for the gift of your Spirit who convicts me and reminds me to humble myself and to think of others more highly than myself. May I reflect your example to my world today.

Additional Scripture for Reflection

Romans 12:2-4

James 4:1-10

Luke 19:1-10

A Day of Reading and Reflection

Scripture for Reflection

Numbers 21:4-9

Then they traveled from Mount Hor by the road to the Red Sea, to go around the land of Edom, but the people became impatient along the way. And the people spoke against God and against Moses, "Why have you brought us up out of Egypt to die in the wilderness, for there is no bread or water, and we detest this worthless food."

So the Lord sent poisonous snakes among the people, and they bit the people; many people of Israel died. Then the people came to Moses and said, "We have sinned, for we have spoken against the Lord and against you. Pray to the Lord that he would take away the snakes from us." So Moses prayed for the people.

The Lord said to Moses, "Make a poisonous snake and set it on a pole. When anyone who is bitten looks at it, he will live." So Moses made a bronze snake and put it on a pole, so that if a snake had bitten someone, when he looked at the bronze snake he lived.

Psalm 107:1-3, 17-22

Give thanks to the Lord, for he is good,
*   and his loyal love endures!*

Let those delivered by the Lord speak out,
*   those whom he delivered from the power of the*
*   enemy,*

and gathered from foreign lands,
*   from east and west,*
*   from north and south.*

They acted like fools in their rebellious ways,
*   and suffered because of their sins.*

They lost their appetite for all food,
*   and they drew near the gates of death.*

They cried out to the Lord in their distress;
*   he delivered them from their troubles.*

He sent them an assuring word and healed them;
*   he rescued them from the pits where they were*
*   trapped.*

Let them give thanks to the Lord for his loyal love,
*   and for the amazing things he has done for*
*   people!*

Let them present thank offerings,
*   and loudly proclaim what he has done!*

Ephesians 2:1-10

And although you were dead in your transgressions and sins, in which you formerly lived according to this world's present path, according to the ruler of the kingdom of the air, the ruler of the spirit that is now energizing the sons of disobedience, among whom all of us also formerly lived out our lives in the cravings of our flesh, indulging the desires of the flesh and the mind, and were by nature children of wrath even as the rest...

But God, being rich in mercy, because of his great love with which he loved us, even though we were dead in transgressions, made us alive together with Christ – by grace you are saved! – and he raised us up with him and seated us with him in the heavenly realms in Christ Jesus, to demonstrate in the coming ages the surpassing wealth of his grace in kindness toward us in Christ Jesus. For by grace you are saved through faith, and this is not from yourselves, it is the gift of God; it is not from works, so that no one can boast. For we are his workmanship, having been created in Christ Jesus for good works that God prepared beforehand so we may do them.

John 3:14-21

Just as Moses lifted up the serpent in the wilderness, so must the Son of Man be lifted up, so that everyone who believes in him may have eternal life."

For this is the way God loved the world: He gave his one and only Son, so that everyone who believes in him will not perish but have eternal life. For God did not send his Son into the world to condemn the world, but that the world should be saved through him. The one who believes in him is not condemned. The one who does not believe has been condemned already, because he has not believed in the name of the one and only Son of God. Now this is the basis for judging: that the light has come into the world and people loved the darkness rather than the light, because their deeds were evil. For everyone who does evil deeds hates the light and does not come to the light, so that their deeds will not be exposed. But the one who practices the truth comes to the light, so that it may be plainly evident that his deeds have been done in God.

Day 18: Some Things Never Change

"What I am saying does not refer to all of you. I know the ones I have chosen. But this is to fulfill the scripture, 'The one who eats my bread has turned against me.' I am telling you this now, before it happens, so that when it happens you may believe that I am he. I tell you the solemn truth, whoever accepts the one I send accepts me, and whoever accepts me accepts the one who sent me."

When he had said these things, Jesus was greatly distressed in spirit, and testified, "I tell you the solemn truth, one of you will betray me." The disciples began to look at one another, worried and perplexed to know which of them he was talking about. One of his disciples, the one Jesus loved, was at the table to the right of Jesus in a place of honor. So Simon Peter gestured to this disciple to ask Jesus who it was he was referring to. Then the disciple whom Jesus loved leaned back against Jesus' chest and asked him, "Lord, who is it?" Jesus replied, "It is the one to whom I will give this piece of bread after I have dipped it in the dish." Then he dipped the piece of bread in the dish and gave it to Judas Iscariot, Simon's son. And after Judas took the piece of bread, Satan entered into him. Jesus said to him, "What you are about to do, do quickly." (Now none of those present at the table understood why Jesus said this to Judas. Some thought that, because Judas had the money box, Jesus was telling him to buy whatever they needed for the feast, or to give something to the poor.) Judas took the piece of bread and went out immediately. (Now it was night.)

When Judas had gone out, Jesus said, "Now the Son of Man is glorified, and God is glorified in him. If God is glorified in him, God will also glorify him in himself, and he will glorify him right away. Children, I am still with you for a little while. You will look for me, and just as I said to the Jewish religious leaders, 'Where I am going you cannot come,' now I tell you the same.

"I give you a new commandment – to love one another. Just as I have loved you, you also are to love one another. Everyone will know by this that you are my disciples – if you have love for one another."

Simon Peter said to him, "Lord, where are you going?" Jesus replied, "Where I am going, you cannot follow me now, but you will follow later." Peter said to him, "Lord, why can't I follow you now? I will lay down my life for you!" Jesus answered, "Will you lay down your life for me? I tell you the solemn truth, the rooster will not crow until you have denied me three times! **John 13:18-38**

This intimate meal that only moments ago included Jesus washing His disciples' feet in so humble a portrait of amazing and unconditional love has veered dramatically, offering what feel like stolen glimpses of the Lord's heart, His soul, His turmoil. But there is an elevated tension, too. To say that the mood has shifted doesn't really convey what's happening around this table right now. Unlike a few moments ago when watching Jesus took my breath away, this feels more like someone just knocked the wind out of me.

The disciples are relaxed, rapt in the company of their Teacher, their friend, their Lord, including Judas. If he is conflicted at all about what he is going to do, it doesn't show. At least not on the outside. Not like it does in his heart, apparently. The heart that Jesus sees. The heart that the Enemy claims.

My heart beats faster at the mention of a betrayer. The disciples look more perplexed, more concerned with who it is than what it means. But even that concern seems, well, a bit cavalier. Peter, normally so outspoken, catches John's eye. A tilt of the head, a raised eyebrow, a subtle signal: *ask Him, John*. Reclining against Jesus, seemingly still wrapped in the intimate, unconditional love of this man who is God who only moments before washed his feet, John asks Him simply, *Lord, who is it?*

Jesus' answer seems straightforward, simple, obvious, even: "It is he to whom I will give this morsel of bread when I have dipped it." He then dips His bread and hands it to Judas.

But there is no reaction from the disciples. No one turns to Judas and demands answers. No one grabs him by his robes, gets in his face and asks him how he can possibly betray this man, this Jesus that they follow, and deeply love. No one gets up and follows Judas to see where he's going or what he's up to.

Why not?

In front of everyone, Judas takes the bread from Jesus. Jesus tells him to go and do what he needs to do quickly and then, Judas leaves.

Why do none of the disciples ask him where he's going?

Why are none of the disciples riled up when Judas takes the incriminating piece of bread?

Why do none of the disciples seem to get it?

I can't help but wonder if it's because it just didn't matter. If it hadn't been Judas, it would have been someone else. Or it would have come about in some other way. But no matter what happened around this table, or anywhere else for that matter, Jesus was going to die. The disciples were about to have plenty enough to wrestle with; they didn't need to be distracted with what Judas was about to do.

And they would each betray Jesus in their own way. No, maybe not to His death. But they would break His heart. They would desert Him. They would deny Him. Each of them, including Judas Iscariot, would have to wrestle with his own demons when his time came.

Judas sold his loyalty for 30 pieces of silver. But how many times have I sold out to the crowd, to the Pharisees of my time, to the easier way for less than that?

The disciples scattered and hid themselves because they were afraid, because they couldn't face the possibility of their own arrest or death because of their friendship with Jesus. But how many times have I hidden my faith or refused to die to myself for the sake of something greater than me because I was afraid?

Peter denied even knowing Jesus. Even though he had walked on water with Jesus. Even though Jesus had healed his mother-in-law. Even though he loved Jesus fiercely. But how many times have I denied my love for Jesus by my words, by my actions, or by my fear?

We all have our own demons with which we need to wrestle. We don't need to take on the sins, the perceived wrongs, the assumed bad choices of others.

Jesus died for Judas just like He died for the 11 other disciples. Just like He died for me. It's not up to me what Judas does with that gift. It's not up to me whether he accepts it or whether he rejects it. It's only up to me to choose what I will do with that gift.

No matter how many times I stumble.

No matter how many times I hide my Light.

No matter how many times I deny Him.

No matter how many times I betray Him.

No matter how many times I sell out.

The gift remains. His gift remains.

And so I get to try again. And again. And again.

Because I am forgiven. Because I am loved.

I am loved intimately, unconditionally, divinely, and extravagantly.

I am loved. This is the gift and I choose not only to receive it and accept it, but to cherish it.

Prayer

Dear Jesus, thank you for your incredible sacrifice. Thank you for dying for me even though you knew that I would mess up often. Thank you for taking away my old, sinful nature and for making me a new creature in you. Help me, Jesus, to live a life worthy of this Truth today.

Additional Scripture for Reflection

2 Corinthians 5:13-17

Romans 6:1-14

Ephesians 2:1-1

Day 17: Great Is Thy Faltering

A dispute also started among them over which of them was to be regarded as the greatest. So Jesus said to them, "The kings of the Gentiles lord it over them, and those in authority over them are called 'benefactors.' Not so with you; instead the one who is greatest among you must become like the youngest, and the leader like the one who serves. For who is greater, the one who is seated at the table, or the one who serves? Is it not the one who is seated at the table? But I am among you as one who serves.

"You are the ones who have remained with me in my trials. Thus I grant to you a kingdom, just as my Father granted to me, that you may eat and drink at my table in my kingdom, and you will sit on thrones judging the twelve tribes of Israel.

"Simon, Simon, pay attention! Satan has demanded to have you all, to sift you like wheat, but I have prayed for you, Simon, that your faith may not fail. When you have turned back, strengthen your brothers." But Peter said to him, "Lord, I am ready to go with you both to prison and to death!" Jesus replied, "I tell you, Peter, the rooster will not crow today until you have denied three times that you know me."

Then Jesus said to them, "When I sent you out with no money bag, or traveler's bag, or sandals, you didn't lack anything, did you?" They replied, "Nothing." He said to them, "But now, the one who has a money bag

must take it, and likewise a traveler's bag too. And the
one who has no sword must sell his cloak and buy
one. For I tell you that this scripture must be fulfilled in
me, 'And he was counted with the transgressors.' For
what is written about me is being fulfilled." So they said,
"Look, Lord, here are two swords." Then he told them,
*"It is enough." **Luke 22:24-38***

Sitting among the disciples, I wonder if they recognize the irony of this moment. As they argue over who will be the greatest among them, they are being sought after by Satan, to be sifted, to be shaken, to be separated and to become less than rather than greater than. They will be sifted like chaff from wheat. With each passing minute of this night, it is clear that things are changing. We are approaching the point of no return and the disciples are not quite tuned in to that.

But rather than admonish, Jesus teaches.

Rather than give up on them, Jesus prays.

Rather than leave them to their own devices or abilities, Jesus equips.

He offers them as much wisdom and understanding as He thinks they will be able to handle. And, lo, the one standing there at the end of Jesus' words is Peter. The same Peter who without hesitation stepped out of the boat at Jesus' bidding even though a storm raged around him. The same Peter who without question lowered his nets at Jesus' bidding even though he had just fished all night and caught nothing. The same Peter who without so much as a stutter or stammer declared Jesus to be the Messiah, the Christ at Jesus' asking.

But tonight, he is not Peter. He is not the Rock. He is not the Cornerstone. And he certainly is not the greatest. Tonight, he is Simon. It's as if he has gone back to who he was before he met Jesus. Before he walked with Jesus in His ministry for the last three years. Before he was changed by Jesus. Tonight, he is, *Simon, Simon*. Such a term, saying the name twice, reflects the love of the speaker. The term reflects the earnestness of the speaker. The term reflects a warning from the speaker, and what a warning Jesus gives, couched in love, yes, but dire nonetheless.

The enemy is on the prowl. He seeks to devour these disciples who claim Jesus as their Lord, as their Messiah. The *you* that Jesus uses when He addresses Simon — Satan demanded to have you — in this moment is plural, not individual. The enemy wants all of them. He wants to shake their faith and separate them from Jesus; sifting them like chaff from wheat.

But Jesus will not allow the enemy to have them.

Jesus won't let the enemy separate them from Him permanently.

He refuses the enemy's request. Instead He prays for Peter. He prays for all of His disciples. He prays for their faith. He prays for their strength.

Jesus knows that Simon will falter. But He knows that Peter will stand. Eventually. Jesus knows Peter is the Rock. But He also knows that Peter will not succeed without Him, without His strength, without His prayers.

My heart beats a little faster as I watch this exchange between Simon and Jesus. How incredible. How amazing is it to know that Jesus prays for us? How incredible that Jesus prays for me, that He sees what's coming and He prays for what I will need in order to face it. Even so, I may, like Simon Peter, falter and suffer.

Oh, the suffering that Simon will experience when he denies his friend, his Lord, his Savior. But, Jesus is already planning for his return, for his renewed strength and for his renewed faith.

Yet why does Jesus fight the enemy for Peter and the other disciples but not for Judas? That seems unfair at first glance, doesn't it? However I can't help but think it has to do with the heart of the man, with his faith and with what he believes. What he *truly* believes.

Judas doesn't believe in the Jesus he knows. He believes in an idea of Jesus that he created. In fact Judas may even be disappointed in the Jesus with whom he has been traveling for the last three years.

Peter believes in Jesus. He believes in Jesus, the man. He believes in Jesus, the Lord. He believes in the miracles. He believes enough to walk on water. He believes enough to lower his nets. He believes enough to lay down his life. Even if he isn't ready to do it right now, he will be. He will and he does.

And I cannot help but wonder, what about me? Do I believe like that? Would I lay down my life like Peter did?

Because I want to.

I want to live a faith like Peter's. I want to walk on water. I want to perform miracles because Jesus said I could. I want to follow Him. I want to know Him. I want to see Him, to know Him the way Peter knows Him, not the way Judas saw Him. I want to know Him because I have walked with Him. Because I have talked with Him. Because I have been in His presence.

135

Because He is Jesus.

And, yes, I want to know that Jesus prays for me.

Watching Peter in this moment, I picture myself as the one to whom Jesus speaks: *Judy, Judy, behold, Satan demanded to have you, that he might sift you like wheat, but I have prayed for you that your faith may not fail; and when you have turned again, strengthen your brethren.*

Jesus prayed for me. I will fight another battle. I will stand strong, because Jesus prayed for me. **For me**.

And, really, is there any bigger miracle than that?

Prayer

Dear Jesus, thank you for who you are and for loving me in spite of who I am, especially when I am so caught up in my own Christianity and sense of "goodness." Thank you, Jesus, for interceding for me then, on the cross, and for interceding for me still, equipping me daily to stand strong in you. Draw me closer to you today, Jesus, so that there is more of you and less of me.

Additional Scripture for Reflection

Psalm 8:3-9

Matthew 17:18-21

Hebrews 7:22-28

Day 16: It Won't Be Enough {until}

Then Jesus said to them, "This night you will all fall away because of me, for it is written:

'I will strike the shepherd,
and the sheep of the flock will be scattered.'

But after I am raised, I will go ahead of you into Galilee." Peter said to him, "If they all fall away because of you, I will never fall away!" Jesus said to him, "I tell you the truth, on this night, before the rooster crows, you will deny me three times." Peter said to him, "Even if I must die with you, I will never deny you." And all the disciples said the same thing. **Matthew 26:31-35**

The end is drawing near. The end of Jesus' ministry. The end of Jesus' time with His disciples. The end of Jesus' life on earth.

It will also be the end of the disciples' confidence. At least temporarily. But they don't know that yet. Right now, as they gather around Jesus in their tightly-knit group, they exude their familiar trust in themselves and in Jesus. Even when Jesus warns them that they will desert Him, that they will abandon Him and one another, they cling to their pride. They cleave to their conviction. They count on their connection to one another. They count on their intimate connection to Jesus.

But it won't be enough.

And, once again, at the center of the group and proclaiming his loyalty the loudest stands Peter. Though he is confronted with the details of his denial, he fiercely denies this possibility. He passionately proclaims that if it comes down to it, he will choose to die rather than deny Jesus. Following his lead, the other disciples echo this pledge of devotion.

But then, why wouldn't they? They have walked with Jesus for three years. They have witnessed His healing miracles. They have watched Him bring a little girl and His good friend, Lazarus, back to life. They have seen Him, and Peter, walk on water and they have witnessed Him rebuke the wind and the waves during a storm.

Yes, Jesus is a man, like them. But Jesus is also divine. He is God. He is the Christ. He is the Son of Man and the Son of God. And they know this. They believe this.

But it won't be enough.

Although He has predicted His death, the disciples do not seem to grasp what is coming. He has been with them. He will always be with them, won't He? Of course He will. But just not in the way they have grown accustomed to. And before they see Him again, in Galilee, they will suffer. They will be sifted by the enemy who will try desperately to defeat them. When the enemy realizes once again that he cannot claim victory against Jesus, he will seek victory against Jesus' followers. He will strike at the disciples. If he cannot win the final battle, the Enemy will take whatever small skirmishes he can claim.

But it won't be enough.

He will strike the shepherd and scatter the sheep. He will seek to plunge Jesus' followers into darkness. He will try to shake their faith. He will attempt to steal their joy, their hope, their confidence in Christ.

Listening to Jesus' words to Peter today, I can't help but think maybe His words are equally intended for me: "You will all fall away. You will be scattered. You will deny me." And I can't help but think these words are equally applicable to everyday moments. Yes, I cannot help but think these words are not intended only for the big moments: *You will all fall away. You will be scattered. You will deny me.* As a follower of Jesus, I am a target for the enemy. He will pursue me passionately. He will seek to sift me and to steal my joy. He will seek to create doubt where I have faith. He will try to cultivate despair where I have hope.

But it won't be enough.

He will win only if I let him.

He will win only if I ignore Jesus' warnings. He will win by default only if I am not intentional. He will win only if I waver. Only if I let him. But I will not let him. Not today.

Today I will proclaim boldly the words of Peter: *Even if I must die with you, I will not deny you!* Today I will stand with Peter and the disciples and draw in close to Jesus and pledge my loyalty to Him. I will tell Him that even though others may fall away, I will not. Even if I must die with you, I will not deny you!

But it won't be enough.

Because even as I proclaim these words I know how hollow they ring. Like the disciples, I have faltered in my friendship with Jesus. And that was when there were no trials. He and I both know that when I face trials, when I struggle, my faith can shift like a wave caught in a gust of wind or fall away like a house of cards.

Even as I promise I will not deny Him, my face, my heart, my faith turn away. But, like Peter and the disciples, I return. I draw close again. I go to Galilee and wait for Him. I seek Him.

But it won't be enough.

Even though I know He will never leave me nor forsake me no matter how many times I abandon Him. Even though I know He loves me no matter how many times I turn tail and run away from Him or hide from Him or deny Him. Even though I know that He defends me, that He prays for me, that He pursues me no matter how often I ignore Him and His truths.

But it won't be enough.

I will have to turn back. I will have to go to Galilee. I will have to seek Him. {again}

And I will find Him. I always find Him.

Because He loves me that much. Because He loves me too much to abandon me to myself or to the world, and especially to the enemy.

Because He loves me. And that is enough. That is more than enough.

That will *always* be enough.

Prayer

Dear Jesus, I am awed by your love and your grace that comes with the blood of your sacrifice. My limited human mind cannot understand how great a love you have for this broken world. Nor can I completely comprehend how great a love you have for me no matter how many times I deny you or desert you. You never stop loving me or pursuing me. You stand on the shore of my life and invite me to come to you and to spend time with you. And then you restore me once again.

Additional Scripture for Reflection

Romans 8:38-39

Isaiah 53:6

James 4:7-10

Day 15: His Death Held So Much Promise

"Do not let your hearts be distressed. You believe in God; believe also in me. There are many dwelling places in my Father's house. Otherwise, I would have told you, because I am going away to make ready a place for you. And if I go and make ready a place for you, I will come again and take you to be with me, so that where I am you may be too. And you know the way where I am going."

Thomas said, "Lord, we don't know where you are going. How can we know the way?" Jesus replied, "I am the way, and the truth, and the life. No one comes to the Father except through me. If you have known me, you will know my Father too. And from now on you do know him and have seen him."

Philip said, "Lord, show us the Father, and we will be content." Jesus replied, "Have I been with you for so long, and you have not known me, Philip? The person who has seen me has seen the Father! How can you say, 'Show us the Father'? Do you not believe that I am in the Father, and the Father is in me? The words that I say to you, I do not speak on my own initiative, but the Father residing in me performs his miraculous deeds. Believe me that I am in the Father, and the Father is in me, but if you do not believe me, believe because of the miraculous deeds themselves. I tell you the solemn truth, the person who believes in me will perform the miraculous deeds that I am doing, and will perform greater deeds than these, because I am going to the Father. And I will do whatever you ask in my name, so that the Father may be glorified in the Son. If you ask me anything in my name, I will do it.

"If you love me, you will obey my commandments. Then I will ask the Father, and he will give you another Advocate to be with you forever – the Spirit of truth, whom the world cannot accept, because it does not see him or know him. But you know him, because he resides with you and will be in you.

"I will not abandon you as orphans, I will come to you. In a little while the world will not see me any longer, but you will see me; because I live, you will live too. You will know at that time that I am in my Father and you are in me and I am in you. The person who has my commandments and obeys them is the one who loves me. The one who loves me will be loved by my Father, and I will love him and will reveal myself to him."

"Lord," Judas (not Judas Iscariot) said, "what has happened that you are going to reveal yourself to us and not to the world?" Jesus replied, "If anyone loves me, he will obey my word, and my Father will love him, and we will come to him and take up residence with him. The person who does not love me does not obey my words. And the word you hear is not mine, but the Father's who sent me.

"I have spoken these things while staying with you. But the Advocate, the Holy Spirit, whom the Father *will send in my name, will teach you everything, and will cause you to remember everything I said to you.*

*"Peace I leave with you; my peace I give to you; I do not give it to you as the world does. Do not let your hearts be distressed or lacking in courage. You heard me say to you, 'I am going away and I am coming back to you.' If you loved me, you would be glad that I am going to the Father, because the Father is greater than I am. I have told you now before it happens, so that when it happens you may believe. I will not speak with you much longer, for the ruler of this world is coming. He has no power over me, but I am doing just what the Father commanded me, so that the world may know that I love the Father. Get up, let us go from here." **John 14:1-31***

I am nervous. No, I am afraid. Even though Jesus tells us not to let our hearts be troubled or to be afraid, the anticipation of what is coming invites this unwelcome fear into my mind, into my heart. He is going away and I don't want Him to. I want Him to stay. I want Him to remain, here, with us, His disciples. I want Him to continue teaching, to continue His miracles.

But that is not why He came.

I know that. He has told us that repeatedly over the last several days. But, still, I don't want Him to go. That He is leaving seems finally to settle on His disciples. Even so, they struggle with His explanations. They pepper Him with questions. How much they understand remains unclear to me. Do they yet know that Jesus will soon be arrested? Do they yet know that He will be beaten? Do they yet know that He will be crucified?

Because that is why He came.

That is why He came. But even though I know that, I still struggle with accepting it. His words echo in my head: *Let not your hearts be troubled*. It seems an impossible request given what is about to happen, given what we must lose in order to gain the more we are promised, given how much He will suffer and how much He will sacrifice. And He does this so that I may live, and so that I truly may know hope.

Because that is why He came.

He came as much *for* me as because of me; because of my sin.

And I wonder. Do the disciples understand this? Do they appreciate the irony of it all? The irony that because we love Him we don't want Him to leave us. We don't want Him to die. The irony that because He loves us He must leave us. He must die.

If we are to live in hope. If we are to experience true joy. If we are to live connected to, in relationship with, our Creator, this man must die. This man who is also my God, who is also my Creator, this Messiah must die.

Because that is why He came.

It's strange how much promise there is in His death.

The promise of forgiveness.

The promise of reconciliation with God.

The promise of living with Jesus always.

The promise of doing great things in the name of Jesus.

The promise of another Helper to guide us and to dwell with us and dwell in us.

The promise of peace.

The promise of grace.

The promise of abundant life.

Because this is why He came.

Even so, how I long for Him to stay. How I long for Him to remain among His believers. He is comfort and He is love. He is amazing grace and unspeakable joy. He is God and He is here. He walks among us. We can see Him. We can hear Him. We can touch Him. We can walk with Him.

He wants me to rejoice because He is returning to the Father. But my heart is heavy. I want Him to stay with me. But it's not about what I want. It's about what I need. With Jesus, it's always about what I need. And I need the promises that can only come with His death, and, more so, with His resurrection. With His leaving this world and returning to the Father.

Because that is why He came.

He came to give me what I need. And in that I will rejoice.

Even though the time is drawing near, I will rejoice.

Even though I am afraid, I will try to let my heart not be troubled.

Even though it hurts, I will stand with Him as He faces humiliation and death.

I will stand at the foot of the cross until He breathes His last.

Yes, I will stand at the foot of the cross and witness His final miracle. The miracle of His death.

Because that is why He came.

Prayer

Dear Jesus, thank you for giving up your place in heaven and coming to our world so that we could know you here for a little while and then know you for eternity. Thank you for reconciling me to the Father and for sending your Helper, our Comforter and Advocate to remain with me here. It is so difficult to recall your suffering because I know that I am responsible for your suffering and I am incredibly thankful for the blood you poured out for me so that I am forgiven and redeemed. I am thankful that I can live a life with you, doing amazing works and changing the world with you and because of you.

Additional Scripture for Reflection

Philippians 2:6-11

Isaiah 53:4-5

Matthew 28:16-20

Day 14: A Vineyard of Love

"I am the true vine and my Father is the gardener. He takes away every branch that does not bear fruit in me. He prunes every branch that bears fruit so that it will bear more fruit. You are clean already because of the word that I have spoken to you. Remain in me, and I will remain in you. Just as the branch cannot bear fruit by itself, unless it remains in the vine, so neither can you unless you remain in me.

"I am the vine; you are the branches. The one who remains in me – and I in him – bears much fruit, because apart from me you can accomplish nothing. If anyone does not remain in me, he is thrown out like a branch, and dries up; and such branches are gathered up and thrown into the fire, and are burned up. If you remain in me and my words remain in you, ask whatever you want, and it will be done for you. My Father is honored by this, that you bear much fruit and show that you are my disciples.

"Just as the Father has loved me, I have also loved you; remain in my love. If you obey my commandments, you will remain in my love, just as I have obeyed my Father's commandments and remain in his love. I have told you these things so that my joy may be in you, and your joy may be complete. My commandment is this – to love one another just as I have loved you. No one has greater love than this – that one lays down his life for his friends. You are my friends if you do what I command you. I no longer call you slaves, because the slave does

not understand what his master is doing. But I have called you friends, because I have revealed to you everything I heard from my Father. You did not choose me, but I chose you and appointed you to go and bear fruit, fruit that remains, so that whatever you ask the Father in my name he will give you. This I command you – to love one another.

"If the world hates you, be aware that it hated me first. If you belonged to the world, the world would love you as its own. However, because you do not belong to the world, but I chose you out of the world, for this reason the world hates you. Remember what I told you, 'A slave is not greater than his master.' If they persecuted me, they will also persecute you. If they obeyed my word, they will obey yours too. But they will do all these things to you on account of my name, because they do not know the one who sent me. If I had not come and spoken to them, they would not be guilty of sin. But they no longer have any excuse for their sin. The one who hates me hates my Father too. If I had not performed among them the miraculous deeds that no one else did, they would not be guilty of sin. But now they have seen the deeds and have hated both me and my Father. Now this happened to fulfill the word that is written in their law, 'They hated me without reason.' When the Advocate comes, whom I will send you from the Father – the Spirit of truth who goes out from the Father – he will testify about me, and you also will testify, because you have been with me from the beginning.

"I have told you all these things so that you will not fall away. They will put you out of the synagogue, yet a time is coming when the one who kills you will think he is offering service to God. They will do these things because they have not known the Father or me. But I have told you these things so that when their time comes, you will remember that I told you about them. "I did not tell you these things from the beginning because I was with you.
John 15:1-27; 16:1-4

Jesus is on the move, leading His disciples from the upper room, from their shared meal, into the darkness of the night. As they follow Him, He talks. He teaches. He warns. As we walk through the now-dark streets of Jerusalem, I feel like I am running, like I cannot quite keep up with Him. But it is His litany of words with which I cannot keep up. He has so much He wants to say and so little time left to say it all. As He speaks, I feel as if I am collecting rare gems. I collect these kernels of truth and hide them away in my heart so they can take root in me, so that they are there when the Helper comes and He can draw them out of me when I need them.

Because I will need them. I will need them often, these words, these truths, these reminders. I know I will need them.

I will need them as I walk through this world as a stranger, for I am but a sojourner.

I will need them as my heavenly Father cuts away every dead branch produced by my efforts to live apart from Him and to love His people by my own efforts.

I will need them when the Father prunes the fruit-bearing branches of my living with the Holy Spirit and developing patience and showing grace and kindness; He will prune me so that I cleave to Him and bear more fruit in His hurting, beautiful world.

I will need them when I am rebuffed, hated, judged by this world because of my relationship, my intimate friendship, with Jesus.

I will need them when I would rather serve myself then serve others.

I will need them. And so I hide them in my heart. And I ponder them. As my feet scrape along the dusty streets of Jerusalem behind Jesus, I ponder them. What does it mean to lay down my life for my friends? What does it mean to be a servant? What does it mean to bear fruit?

What does it mean to abide in Jesus, to abide in His love? Those are the words that stop me in my tracks. Those are the words that take my breath away here on the darkened streets of Jerusalem. Even as Jesus moves toward the cross, toward His death, He offers me life. He offers me joy, His joy, abundant and full, spilling over into every part of my life. He offers me love. And He invites me to abide there, to abide in Him.

And I take Him up on His offer even before I understand fully what it means or what it will look like.

What does it look like to abide in the love of Jesus? What does it look like to abide in Jesus?

Clearly, if I abide in Jesus, there will be fruit: love, joy, peace, patience, kindness, goodness, faithfulness, gentleness and

151

self-control. Clearly, these are possible only as one conforms to the character of Christ.

Clearly, if I abide in Jesus, I will defer to Him. When I am faced with a choice or a decision, I will consider what love would do. I will consider what a servant would do.

Clearly, if I abide in Jesus, I will dwell with Him. I will stay with Him. I will live in this world, but I will dwell with Christ. I will live as a citizen of heaven. I will live as a sojourner.

Clearly, if I abide in Jesus, I will follow Him. Just as I follow Him now, through the streets of Jerusalem, to the Mount of Olives, to the Upper Room, to the Garden of Gethsemane, to the cross. I will follow Him. I will listen to Him. I will draw near to Him. I will proclaim Him. I will love Him.

I will love Him.

I will lay down my life for Him.

I will lay down my life so that I may have His. And by so doing I may abide in Him daily.

Prayer

Dear Jesus, thank you for the invitation and the gift of abiding in you so that you are a place of refuge and a place of renewal. Thank you for the gift of abiding in you so that I can bear fruit in this broken, beautiful, hurting world. Thank you, too, for calling me friend and for willingly laying your life down for me. I can scarcely comprehend all that means, that my God and Creator would so willingly die for me. I ask you today to help me love others as you love me and to heed the reminders of your Holy Spirit so that I might bear witness to your glory and your truth.

Additional Scripture for Reflection

Psalm 91:1-4

Psalm 119:9-16

Galatians 5:22-23

Day 13: I'm Desperate, So I'm Asking

But now I am going to the one who sent me, and not one of you is asking me, 'Where are you going?' Instead your hearts are filled with sadness because I have said these things to you. But I tell you the truth, it is to your advantage that I am going away. For if I do not go away, the Advocate will not come to you, but if I go, I will send him to you. And when he comes, he will prove the world wrong concerning sin and righteousness and judgment –

concerning sin, because they do not believe in me; concerning righteousness, because I am going to the Father and you will see me no longer; and concerning judgment, because the ruler of this world has been condemned.

"I have many more things to say to you, but you cannot bear them now. But when he, the Spirit of truth, comes, he will guide you into all truth. For he will not speak on his own authority, but will speak whatever he hears, and will tell you what is to come. He will glorify me, because he will receive from me what is mine and will tell it to you. Everything that the Father has is mine; that is why I said the Spirit will receive from me what is mine and will tell it to you. In a little while you will see me no longer; again after a little while, you will see me."

Then some of his disciples said to one another, "What is the meaning of what he is saying, 'In a little while you will not see me; again after a little while, you will see me,' and, 'because I am going to the Father'?" So they kept on repeating, "What is the meaning of what he says, 'In a little while'? We do not understand what he is talking about."

Jesus could see that they wanted to ask him about these things, so he said to them, "Are you asking each other about this – that I said, 'In a little while you will not see me; again after a little while, you will see me'? I tell you the solemn truth, you will weep and wail, but the world will rejoice; you will be sad, but your sadness will turn into joy. When a woman gives birth, she has distress because her time has come, but when her child is born, she no longer remembers the suffering because of her joy that a human being has been born into the world. So also you have sorrow now, but I will see you again, and your hearts will rejoice, and no one will take your joy away from you. At that time you will ask me nothing. I tell you the solemn truth, whatever you ask the Father in my name he will give you. Until now you have not asked for anything in my name. Ask and you will receive it, so that your joy may be complete.

"I have told you these things in obscure figures of speech; a time is coming when I will no longer speak to you in obscure figures, but will tell you plainly about the Father. At that time you will ask in my name, and I do not say that I will ask the Father on your behalf. For the Father himself loves you, because you have loved me and have believed that I came from God. I came from the

Father and entered into the world, but in turn, I am leaving the world and going back to the Father."

His disciples said, "Look, now you are speaking plainly and not in obscure figures of speech! Now we know that you know everything and do not need anyone to ask you anything. Because of this we believe that you have come from God."

*Jesus replied, "Do you now believe? Look, a time is coming – and has come – when you will be scattered, each one to his own home, and I will be left alone. Yet I am not alone, because my Father is with me. I have told you these things so that in me you may have peace. In the world you have trouble and suffering, but take courage – I have conquered the world." **John 16:5-33***

Have you ever noticed the closer you draw to Jesus, the harder you pursue Him, the greater the Resistance you hit? I'm not talking about mild pushback. I'm not talking about feeling torn between spending time with Jesus versus doing the dishes or folding the laundry.

I'm talking about true Resistance. I'm talking about straight out, no-holds-barred spiritual warfare. The kind of Resistance that only the enemy is capable of bringing against a follower of Jesus. The kind of struggle that wears you down. The kind of battle that brings you to your knees, that bring you to a desperate need for prayer.

That is where I am right now as I write these words.

Since starting this journey with Jesus, since following Jesus to Jerusalem these many days, I have noticed that some days feel like walking under water. Some days require incredible effort to defeat the enemy's efforts to derail me, to drive me into the darkness of doubt or despair.

And, honestly, sometimes I not only falter, I fall. I fall for his lies. I fall into his traps. I fall into the despair to which he lures me. I not only give him a foothold, I throw open the door. Without realizing it, I give him carte blanche to trip me up, one angry thought, one angry word at a time.

It was the anger, and my angry words, that finally woke me up to the battle today. Anger bubbles and boils beneath the surface, much too close to the surface. It caused me finally to pause and to ask my husband, "What is going on with me?"

Without missing a beat, he replied, "It's spiritual."

I stared at him blankly, not because I didn't believe him or think that this was a real possibility, but because I hadn't considered it. He added with conviction, "It means we need a whole lot more prayer."

Prayer.

It's one of the biggest weapons we have against the enemy.

And during this journey with Jesus, He has reminded me of this often. In fact, He has told His disciples, He has told Peter and He has told me, that because of the threat of the enemy, He prays for His followers. He intercedes for us. He intercedes for *me*. But more importantly, Jesus tells us again and again, "Whatever you ask of the Father in my name, He will give it to you."

I remember when I first encountered those words. I thought, really? Anything I ask in Jesus' name, God will give to me? Granted, I was much younger. Less wise. But it was enticing to say the least because I pictured God as a giver of gifts, a bestower of blessings. I've matured a lot since then. I realize that God is not an over-indulgent grandparent standing by to spoil me with whatever I want. Rather He is a refuge and a mighty fortress, and He is the one who does battle on my behalf. If I ask Him to.

If I ask. If I come to Him and ask Him to fight this battle for me, in Jesus' name, He will fight for me. And He will win.

The enemy is wily. But God is mighty.

The enemy is a liar. But God is truth.

The enemy is darkness. But God is light.

The enemy is desperate. But God is divine. He is all-knowing and ever-present and all-powerful.

And sometimes, I forget that these characteristics apply only to Him. Only to God. Only to the great I Am. Sometimes, I forget that the enemy does not know my heart. He does not know my mind. He does not know my purpose in this world. Yes, he knows my mistakes and my tendencies. And he will use those to his gain. But no matter what the enemy can do, he is not God. He is *not* equal to God.

He is not equal to God. Actually he was *created* by God.

In fact, he was *defeated* by God. He lost to Jesus.

And I can defeat him. Through prayer. In Christ. With God.

That is why today I paused. And I prayed.

Intimate, pleading prayers. Asking Jesus to be my refuge and to fight this battle for me.

Contrite, confessional prayers. Admitting to Jesus that I have lost sight of Him in my day-to-day. That I've gotten too comfortable and too complacent.

Desperate, heart-felt, intentional prayers. Seeking God's power and asking God's protection.

Humble, on-my-face, crying-out-to-God prayers. Calling on God's promises and claiming them as truth.

Praying constantly. Praying without ceasing.

Is this skirmish over?

Not likely.

Even so, I continue this journey with Jesus. I follow Him to Jerusalem and I heed His words. I absorb them. I apply them. Especially the ones that repeatedly remind me that whatever I ask of God in Jesus' name, I will receive.

And so I pray. And I do battle and cleave to my God. And I pray some more.

And in the name of Jesus, the mighty, powerful, victorious name of Jesus, I bid the enemy go, leave me, go back from whence he came. I pray. And he flees.

And I walk with Jesus.

I follow Him through the streets of Jerusalem.

I listen to His words.

And I refuse to let the enemy insert himself in between me and Jesus.

Instead, I take heart.

I take heart and know that Jesus has overcome this world and I know that Jesus won the Victory.

And I know that I am His.

I belong to Jesus.

And so I take my heart and I give it to Jesus. I let Him defend it. I let Him protect it.

Because I am His.

Prayer

Dear Jesus, thank you for the strength you give and the refuge you provide and for the power you offer to those who love you and call upon your name. Thank you for defeating the enemy and for the armor of God that is mine daily to wear as I enter into each day's tasks. How amazing it is to know that the Creator of the universe hears my prayers when I speak them in your might and powerful name.

Additional Scripture for Reflection

Ephesians 6:10-18

John 16:32-33

John 14:12-14

A Day of Reading and Reflection

Scripture for Reflection

Jeremiah 31:31-34

"Indeed, a time is coming," says the Lord, "when I will make a new covenant with the people of Israel and Judah. It will not be like the old covenant that I made with their ancestors when I delivered them from Egypt. For they violated that covenant, even though I was like a faithful husband to them," says the Lord. "But I will make a new covenant with the whole nation of Israel after I plant them back in the land," says the Lord. "I will put my law within them and write it on their hearts and minds. I will be their God and they will be my people.

"People will no longer need to teach their neighbors and relatives to know me. For all of them, from the least important to the most important, will know me," says the Lord. "For I will forgive their sin and will no longer call to mind the wrong they have done."

Psalm 51:1-12

For the music director; a psalm of David, written when Nathan the prophet confronted him after David's affair with Bathsheba.

Have mercy on me, O God, because of your loyal love!

Because of your great compassion, wipe away my rebellious acts!

Wash away my wrongdoing!
   Cleans me of my sin!

For I am aware of my rebellious acts;
   I am forever conscious of my sin.

Against you — you above all — I have sinned;
   I have done what is evil in your sight.
   So you are just when you confront me;
   you are right when you condemn me.

Look, I was guilty of sin from birth,
   a sinner the moment my mother conceived me.

Look, you desire integrity in the inner man;
   you want me to possess wisdom.

Sprinkle me with water and I will be pure;
   wash me and I will be whiter than snow.

Grant me the ultimate joy of being forgiven!
   May the bones you crushed rejoice!

Hide your face from my sins!
   Wipe away all my guilt!

Create for me a pure heart, O God!
   Renew a resolute spirit within me!

Do not reject me!
   Do not take your Holy Spirit away from me!
   Let me again experience the joy of your deliverance!
   Sustain me by giving me the desire to obey!

Hebrews 5:5-10

*So also Christ did not glorify himself in becoming high priest, but the one who glorified him was God, who said to him, "**You are my Son! Today I have fathered you**," as also in another place God says, "**You are a priest forever in the order of Melchizedek**." During his earthly life Christ offered both requests and supplications, with loud cries and tears, to the one who was able to save him from death and he was heard because of his devotion. Although he was a son, he learned obedience through the things he suffered. And by being perfected in this way, he became the source of eternal salvation to all who obey him, and he was designated by God as high priest **in the order of Melchizedek**.*

John 12:20-33

Now some Greeks were among those who had gone up to worship at the feast. So these approached Philip, who was from Bethsaida in Galilee, and requested, "Sir, we would like to see Jesus." Philip went and told Andrew, and they both went and told Jesus. Jesus replied, "The time has come for the Son of Man to be glorified. I tell you the solemn truth, unless a kernel of wheat falls into the ground and dies, it remains by itself alone. But if it dies, it produces much grain. The one who loves his life destroys it, and the one who hates his life in this world guards it for eternal life. If anyone wants to serve me, he must follow me, and where I am, my servant will be too. If anyone serves me, the Father will honor him.

"Now my soul is greatly distressed. And what should I say? 'Father, deliver me from this hour'? No, but for this very reason I have come to this hour. Father, glorify your name." Then a voice came from heaven, "I have glorified it, and I will glorify it again." The crowd that stood there and heard the voice said that it had thundered. Others said that an angel had spoken to him. Jesus said, "This voice has not come for my benefit but for yours. Now is the judgment of this world; now the ruler of this world will be driven out. And I, when I am lifted up from the earth, will draw all people to myself." (Now he said this to indicate clearly what kind of death he was going to die.)

Day 12: The Glory of Prayer

When Jesus had finished saying these things, he looked upward to heaven and said, "Father, the time has come. Glorify your Son, so that your Son may glorify you – just as you have given him authority over all humanity, so that he may give eternal life to everyone you have given him. Now this is eternal life – that they know you, the only true God, and Jesus Christ, whom you sent. I glorified you on earth by completing the work you gave me to do. And now, Father, glorify me at your side with the glory I had with you before the world was created.

"I have revealed your name to the men you gave me out of the world. They belonged to you, and you gave them to me, and they have obeyed your word. Now they understand that everything you have given me comes from you, because I have given them the words you have given me. They accepted them and really understand that I came from you, and they believed that you sent me. I am praying on behalf of them. I am not praying on behalf of the world, but on behalf of those you have given me, because they belong to you. Everything I have belongs to you, and everything you have belongs to me, and I have been glorified by them. I am no longer in the world, but they are in the world, and I am coming to you. Holy Father, keep them safe in your name that you have given me, so that they may be one just as we are one. When I was with them I kept them safe and watched over them in

your name that you have given me. Not one of them was lost except the one destined for destruction, so that the scripture could be fulfilled. But now I am coming to you, and I am saying these things in the world, so they may experience my joy completed in themselves. I have given them your word, and the world has hated them, because they do not belong to the world, just as I do not belong to the world. I am not asking you to take them out of the world, but that you keep them safe from the evil one. They do not belong to the world just as I do not belong to the world. Set them apart in the truth; your word is truth. Just as you sent me into the world, so I sent them into the world. And I set myself apart on their behalf, so that they too may be truly set apart.

"I am not praying only on their behalf, but also on behalf of those who believe in me through their testimony, that they will all be one, just as you, Father, are in me and I am in you. I pray that they will be in us, so that the world will believe that you sent me. The glory you gave to me I have given to them, that they may be one just as we are one – I in them and you in me – that they may be completely one, so that the world will know that you sent me, and you have loved them just as you have loved me.

"Father, I want those you have given me to be with me where I am, so that they can see my glory that you gave me because you loved me before the creation of the world. Righteous Father, even if the world does not know you, I know you, and these men know that you sent me. I

*made known your name to them, and I will continue to make it known, so that the love you have loved me with may be in them, and I may be in them." **John 17:1-26***

As we lounge around the table listening to Jesus, having finished an intimate meal together, I want to stay in this Upper Room forever. Life feels the best it has for me in a long time in spite of Jesus' words that His betrayer sits around this table with us even now. Maybe if we all stay squirreled away in this room we can continue as is and all the predictions Jesus made about His death won't have to happen. Even as I think these things in my heart I know in my head that Jesus is not meant to be ours alone. That isn't why He's here in Jerusalem. Even so, I yearn to hold on to this time just a little while longer. And as Jesus finishes up telling us that though we are scattered the Father remains with Him to the end of what's coming, it seems He indulges my desire to remain here with Him.

He turns His eyes to heaven and begins to pray and this room becomes even more intimate in light of His words. I sense a warmth that builds from within as He pours out a prayer of love, of hope, of truth, and of blessing on all of His disciples (except for Judas, who left during dinner).

I don't know if you've ever had the incredibly powerful experience of having someone pray over you or for you, but there is nothing like it for me. To hear someone raise words of prayer meant specifically for and about you is intensely intimate, shrinking the space between you by inviting God into the space to knit your hearts together in love and hope.

167

Imagine, then, what it's like to listen to Jesus pray for you. To speak His heart to the Father, asking the Father to watch over you, to protect you from the enemy, to bring you into oneness with Jesus and His Father. Even as He prepares to leave this room and enter into His final act of love and surrender, Jesus focuses on those He loves. That He pauses in the midst of the pressing circumstances awaiting all of us on the other side of the door once more demonstrates the depth of His love for us.

The words of His prayer wrap around me as He prays first for Himself, revealing even more about who He is and how His reason for coming into the world — to glorify the Father — provides me encouragement to do likewise on my journey. As He moves into praying for the 11 who remain with Him, I feel tears welling up, starting in my heart and moving to my eyes. He is both gentle, in His desire for the disciples' protection and sanctification, and mighty, in His request to fortify and empower them as they take up their mission to speak boldly and proclaim the truth of Jesus and the Word.

But it is when He moves into interceding on my behalf that I am moved to my deepest sense of gratitude, awe, and emotion. My human mind cannot completely grasp all that He asks of the Father for me, but it reminds me I am a daughter of the King and I absolutely am created by God, for God, and in the image of God.

The glory that you have given me I have given to them, that they may be one even as we are one, I in them and you in me (ESV). No, I am not equal to Jesus; He is fully God after all. But that doesn't stop Him from praying His glory over me and my life, inviting me to be a part of God's work in this world. And because He knows this isn't something I can accomplish in my own strength or by my own efforts, He prays His power, His life, and His glory, into me, weaving it into me like a vine weaves around and becomes one with the branches that eventually bear fruit.

But He doesn't stop there. He reminds me how deeply I am loved by the Creator — *I made known to them your name, and I will continue to make it known, that the love with which you have loved me may be in them, and I in them (ESV).* There is no way I can truly understand these words, to understand what it means to have the love of God, the love with which God loves Jesus, in me.

That I too often listen to the world's estimation of me or question my worth, ability, or purpose is inconceivable as I digest these words of prayer spoken by Jesus over me right now. I am reminded that Jesus has almost never once addressed the questions of those who have engaged Him during His ministry; rather, He has addressed their hearts. Even as He faces the end of His journey and mission in this world He created, He cares so much for my heart He intercedes in prayer to the Father for me.

As Jesus closes out His prayer, I whisper my own small but desperate prayer: please, God, may I not forget the truths of Jesus' words spoken in this room tonight. I look into Jesus' face, my eyes on His, and speak three simple, heartfelt words, *thank you, Jesus.*

Prayer

Dear Jesus, I give You thanks for seeing me, all of me, and accepting me anyway. You see my heart and You make it Your dwelling place; Your Spirit speaks wisdom to me, guiding me on the path You have for me. Even more, Your Spirit intercedes for me with the Father. I am reconciled to You and the Father through the Spirit. Thank you for leaving us the Spirit and for providing Your Word to encourage me and to guide me. May I always seek first the kingdom and presence of God in all that I do.

Additional Scripture for Reflection

Ephesians 6:10-20
1 Samuel 12:6-25
Romans 8:18-30

Day 11: Like a Thief in the Night

Then Jesus went with them to a place called Gethsemane, and he said to the disciples, "Sit here while I go over there and pray." He took with him Peter and the two sons of Zebedee, and became anguished and distressed. Then he said to them, "My soul is deeply grieved, even to the point of death. Remain here and stay awake with me." Going a little farther, he threw himself down with his face to the ground and prayed, "My Father, if possible, let this cup pass from me! Yet not what I will, but what you will." Then he came to the disciples and found them sleeping. He said to Peter, "So, couldn't you stay awake with me for one hour? Stay awake and pray that you will not fall into temptation. The spirit is willing, but the flesh is weak." He went away a second time and prayed, "My Father, if this cup cannot be taken away unless I drink it, your will must be done." He came again and found them sleeping; they could not keep their eyes open. So leaving them again, he went away and prayed for the third time, saying the same thing once more. Then he came to the disciples and said to them, "Are you still sleeping and resting? Look, the hour is approaching, and the Son of Man is betrayed into the hands of sinners. Get up, let us go. Look! My betrayer is approaching!"

While he was still speaking, Judas, one of the twelve, arrived. With him was a large crowd armed with swords and clubs, sent by the chief priests and elders of the people. (Now the betrayer had given them a sign,

171

saying, "The one I kiss is the man. Arrest him!") Immediately he went up to Jesus and said, "Greetings, Rabbi," and kissed him. Jesus said to him, "Friend, do what you are here to do." Then they came and took hold of Jesus and arrested him. But one of those with Jesus grabbed his sword, drew it out, and struck the high priest's slave, cutting off his ear. Then Jesus said to him, "Put your sword back in its place! For all who take hold of the sword will die by the sword. Or do you think that I cannot call on my Father, and that he would send me more than twelve legions of angels right now? How then would the scriptures that say it must happen this way be fulfilled?" At that moment Jesus said to the crowd, "Have you come out with swords and clubs to arrest me like you would an outlaw? Day after day I sat teaching in the temple courts, yet you did not arrest me. But this has happened so that the scriptures of the prophets would be fulfilled." Then all the disciples left him and fled.
Matthew 26:36-56

His time has finally come.

Taking His three closest friends with Him, Jesus goes to Gethsemane. He is deeply troubled. He is deeply sorrowful. His disciples are deeply sleepy. He prays; they sleep. Three times He prays. Three times they sleep.

In the shadows of one of the olive trees I sit, and I watch, and I cry.

But I do not sleep.

Because tonight is the night.

Tonight Jesus prays.

Tonight Jesus pours out His heart to His Father.

Tonight Jesus cries.

Tonight Jesus is seized. Like a thief in the night. Like a threat.

Tonight Jesus drinks the cup that is set before Him.

In spite of His fear, He drinks the cup.

In spite of His sorrow, He drinks the cup.

In spite of His deep and intimate connection to the Father, He drinks the cup.

Even though He is God, He drinks the cup.

Because it is the only way, He drinks the cup.

Because of His love for us, He drinks the cup.

Even so I can see His pain. I watch Him wrestle with what is before Him. I watch Him pray alone. I watch Him stand alone. I watch Him drink the cup alone.

And I sense with a sharp, deeply piercing conviction my weakness. I am powerless to stop what is unfolding before me. I am powerless to change what must happen. I am powerless to change my life without His death.

At long last, the great crowd arrives bearing swords and clubs, bearing anger and fear. As they move to seize my Savior, Peter, impetuous Peter, draws his sword to defend Jesus. And I wonder if he recognizes that his moment has passed. I wonder if he realizes his missed opportunity to stand with Jesus by kneeling with Him and by praying for Him.

173

This man who so passionately loves Jesus could not stay awake. He was overcome by this world, by its temptations, by his weakness. Perhaps it is this realization that causes Peter to strike with his sword; one final effort to make up for his inability to keep watch when Jesus asked him to.

And I wonder how many times I substitute my own plans or actions because I did not heed Jesus' words. Because I did not follow His plan. Because I was too afraid, too tired, too overcome by the world to keep watch or to pray. I wonder how many times I, like Peter, have missed the opportunity to pray with Jesus in the garden.

Here in this garden, Jesus is God, but He is also very much a man. He is capable of fear and longing and pain. He is capable of needing the strength of His friends in His hour of need. But because He is God, He does not hold their humanness against them. He does not resent their weakness. In fact, it is why He came. It is why when Peter strikes with his sword, Jesus says simply, "No, not like this."

Unlike His disciples whose spirit is willing and whose flesh is weak, Jesus ultimately is willing in both spirit and flesh to fulfill His purpose.

Unlike His disciples who flee in the face of this crowd, Jesus surrenders, not only *to* them, but *for* them; not only to them, but to His Father. Not only to them, but to us. *For us.*

For all of us. For you. For me.

Jesus surrenders for all of us.

His time has come. And like His disciples, I fall away. I flee. I flee with my pain and with my gratitude.

And I cry.

And I wait.

Because this is not the end. This is not done.

And even when it is done, that will not be the end.

It will be the beginning. The new beginning we all need.

But first, we must endure to the end.

Prayer

Dear Jesus, sometimes there are barely words to tell you how grateful I am for your incredible and amazing sacrifice. Sometimes, like now, when I allow myself to see, truly see you in the garden, on your knees, in your anguish, I am speechless. I am speechless because it is too easy to forget who you are. Too easy to forget that you are as much a man as you are God in that moment and that you knew pain and fear and sorrow. Thank you, Jesus, for choosing to drink the cup so I did not have to.

Additional Scripture for Reflection

Hebrews 12:1-3

1 Peter 3:8-15

John 6:32-40

Day 10: Never Out of Control

When he had said these things, Jesus went out with his disciples across the Kidron Valley. There was an orchard there, and he and his disciples went into it. (Now Judas, the one who betrayed him, knew the place too, because Jesus had met there many times with his disciples.) So Judas obtained a squad of soldiers and some officers of the chief priests and Pharisees. They came to the orchard with lanterns and torches and weapons.

Then Jesus, because he knew everything that was going to happen to him, came and asked them, "Who are you looking for?" They replied, "Jesus the Nazarene." He told them, "I am he." (Now Judas, the one who betrayed him, was standing there with them.) So when Jesus said to them, "I am he," they retreated and fell to the ground. Then Jesus asked them again, "Who are you looking for?" And they said, "Jesus the Nazarene." Jesus replied, "I told you that I am he. If you are looking for me, let these men go." He said this to fulfill the word he had spoken, "I have not lost a single one of those whom you gave me."

Then Simon Peter, who had a sword, pulled it out and struck the high priest's slave, cutting off his right ear. (Now the slave's name was Malchus.) But Jesus said to Peter, "Put your sword back into its sheath! Am I not to drink the cup that the Father has given me?"

Then the squad of soldiers with their commanding officer and the officers of the Jewish leaders arrested Jesus and tied him up. They brought him first to Annas, for he was the father-in-law of Caiaphas, who was high priest that year. (Now it was Caiaphas who had advised the Jewish leaders that it was to their advantage that one man die for the people.)

Simon Peter and another disciple followed them as they brought Jesus to Annas. (Now the other disciple was acquainted with the high priest, and he went with Jesus into the high priest's courtyard.) But Simon Peter was left standing outside by the door. So the other disciple who was acquainted with the high priest came out and spoke to the slave girl who watched the door, and brought Peter inside. The girl who was the doorkeeper said to Peter, "You're not one of this man's disciples too, are you?" He replied, "I am not." (Now the slaves and the guards were standing around a charcoal fire they had made, warming themselves because it was cold. Peter also was standing with them, warming himself.) **John 18:1-18**

I stand beside Peter in the garden. I watch him take his sword and swing it wildly, taking off the ear of the high priest's servant. His desire to protect Jesus, to stave off what is coming, what is inevitable, is clear even in the dark of the garden. But Jesus is quick to act, to counteract Peter's lashing out. Jesus stops him and assures Peter that even now, He is still in control.

Jesus remains in control even as Malchus' ear is cut off by Peter.

Jesus remains in control even as Judas Iscariot leads a band of soldiers into this sacred space to arrest Him.

Jesus remains in control despite the dire circumstances.

Even as He is bound and led away by this band of soldiers, Jesus provides reassurance to His disciples and assurances to Peter. The same Peter who will follow Him even if at a distance. The same Peter who will watch what happens from the shadows. The same Peter who will deny Him only a short time from now. As Jesus and another disciple enter the courtyard of the high priest, Peter stands outside. Peter waits.

While he waits does he glance around? Does he hide his face? Does he consider running?

While he waits does he feel alone? Even in the midst of the crowd that is growing around Him, does he feel alone? Does he feel abandoned? Is he afraid?

While he waits does he believe that Jesus is really still in control?

Watching him and watching Jesus, do I?

After only a few moments, the other disciple approaches the door, speaks to a young servant girl and gets Peter inside the courtyard. I wonder as I watch him, does he long to be somewhere else? Anywhere else? Anywhere but here? I think perhaps he may. How can he not? This is his friend, his Lord, his Savior. This is the Messiah, the King of Kings. This is Jesus. I think perhaps he must. Why else does he not hesitate in his denial of being one of Jesus' disciples?

But here he is. Inside the courtyard and gathered around the fire with the servants and the soldiers. One other disciple is here.

But, really, Peter is alone. In the midst of this crowd. With Jesus standing not far off. Standing by the warm, cozy fire. Peter is alone.

He seems to shiver. And though it is cold, I cannot help but think that he does not shiver from the chill. I cannot help but think that he shivers from fear. And from loneliness. And because he is beginning to understand what is happening. He is beginning to understand what is coming.

Standing close to the fire does little to take the chill from my bones. It does little to soothe the ache that is forming deep in my stomach or the one deep in my heart. Standing close to the fire I shake and wrap my arms tightly around myself to quell the shivers of fear and shame that build inside me. I look around at the faces huddled close to the fire and wonder if in the glow of the dancing, flickering firelight they can see the tears that spill onto my cheeks as I fold into myself.

Even though I feel the body heat from those pressed against me. Even though I am jostled by the movements of these strangers. Even though I know I am surrounded by a growing crowd of soldiers and servants. Even so, I feel small. I feel alone.

It is a bone-deep loneliness and longing.

I can see Jesus. He is standing right there, not more than a few yards from me. And yet He is so far away. I wonder if He would hear me if I whispered His name. I'm pretty sure He would. Because He is Jesus; He is God.

But right now, in this moment, what is He thinking? What does He need? Not the God-side part of Jesus, but the human side of Him. It feels almost selfish to be so focused on my longing, on my loneliness, on my fear right now.

Is He tired?

Is He thirsty?

Does He feel alone?

Does He feel abandoned?

Does He feel afraid?

This Jesus who created the world. This Jesus who created man. This Jesus who is the only begotten son.

Does He feel afraid?

He knows His purpose. He's known it since before the world began. But does that mean He doesn't feel what I feel right now? That He doesn't feel a hundred times more than what I'm feeling. He is fully God and fully man. It is a mystery I do not understand, but one that I believe.

And as I shiver by the fire, I long to comfort Him. I long to take His hand in mine and stand beside Him. I long to free Him.

If only I were not the one who so desperately needed freeing.

If only I were not the one who had made His sacrifice necessary.

And so I do the only thing I can do in this moment. I stand and watch. And wait. And cry.

I cry for Jesus.

I cry for Peter.

I cry for myself. For the part I've played in all of this.

I cry.

Prayer

Dear Jesus, when I stand this close to you and watch what you are doing so willingly for this broken world and for me, I am overwhelmed. I am overcome with sorrow, but also with gratitude. Overflowing, incredible gratitude and awe. These moments and this journey remind me how much this life I live with abundant grace and blessing cost you. And I am so incredibly thankful dear Jesus, for that kind of love. For that kind of example of unconditional love. An unconditional love that I cannot truly understand but that I cherish.

Additional Scripture for Reflection

Isaiah 58:7-12

Philippians 2:1-11

Psalm 51

Day 9: Bearing the Burden of Love

Then they went to a place called Gethsemane, and Jesus said to his disciples, "Sit here while I pray." He took Peter, James, and John with him, and became very troubled and distressed. He said to them, "My soul is deeply grieved, even to the point of death. Remain here and stay alert." Going a little farther, he threw himself to the ground and prayed that if it were possible the hour would pass from him. He said, "Abba, Father, all things are possible for you. Take this cup away from me. Yet not what I will, but what you will." Then he came and found them sleeping, and said to Peter, "Simon, are you sleeping? Couldn't you stay awake for one hour? Stay awake and pray that you will not fall into temptation. The spirit is willing, but the flesh is weak." He went away again and prayed the same thing. When he came again he found them sleeping; they could not keep their eyes open. And they did not know what to tell him. He came a third time and said to them, "Are you still sleeping and resting? Enough of that! The hour has come. Look, the Son of Man is betrayed into the hands of sinners. Get up, let us go. Look! My betrayer is approaching!"

Right away, while Jesus was still speaking, Judas, one of the twelve, arrived. With him came a crowd armed with swords and clubs, sent by the chief priests and experts in the law and elders. (Now the betrayer had given them a sign, saying, "The one I kiss is the man.

Arrest him and lead him away under guard.") When Judas arrived, he went up to Jesus immediately and said, "Rabbi!" and kissed him. Then they took hold of him and arrested him. One of the bystanders drew his sword and struck the high priest's slave, cutting off his ear. Jesus said to them, "Have you come with swords and clubs to arrest me like you would an outlaw? Day after day I was with you, teaching in the temple courts, yet you did not arrest me. But this has happened so that the scriptures would be fulfilled." Then all the disciples left him and fled. A young man was following him, wearing only a linen cloth. They tried to arrest him, but he ran off naked, leaving his linen cloth behind.

Then they led Jesus to the high priest, and all the chief priests and elders and experts in the law came together. And Peter had followed him from a distance, up to the high priest's courtyard. He was sitting with the guards and warming himself by the fire. The chief priests and the whole Sanhedrin were looking for evidence against Jesus so that they could put him to death, but they did not find anything. Many gave false testimony against him, but their testimony did not agree. Some stood up and gave this false testimony against him: "We heard him say, 'I will destroy this temple made with hands and in three days build another not made with hands.'" Yet even on this point their testimony did not agree. Then the high priest stood up before them and asked Jesus, "Have you no answer? What is this that they are testifying against you?" But he was silent and did not answer. Again the high priest questioned him, "Are you the Christ, the Son of the Blessed One?" "I am," said Jesus, "and you will

183

see the Son of Man sitting at the right hand of the Power and coming with the clouds of heaven." Then the high priest tore his clothes and said, "Why do we still need witnesses? You have heard the blasphemy! What is your verdict?" They all condemned him as deserving death. Then some began to spit on him, and to blindfold him, and to strike him with their fists, saying, "Prophesy!" The guards also took him and beat him.

Now while Peter was below in the courtyard, one of the high priest's slave girls came by. When she saw Peter warming himself, she looked directly at him and said, "You also were with that Nazarene, Jesus." But he denied it: "I don't even understand what you're talking about!" Then he went out to the gateway, and a rooster crowed. When the slave girl saw him, she began again to say to the bystanders, "This man is one of them." But he denied it again. A short time later the bystanders again said to Peter, "You must be one of them, because you are also a Galilean." Then he began to curse, and he swore with an oath, "I do not know this man you are talking about!" Immediately a rooster crowed a second time. Then Peter remembered what Jesus had said to him: "Before a rooster crows twice, you will deny me three times." And he broke down and wept. **Mark 14:32-72**

Jesus betrayed into the hands of sinners. As I stand with James, John and Peter, I marvel at these words and at the incredible irony they hold. That Jesus, who came to save sinners, to forgive them, to redeem them, to die for them, is betrayed into their very hands.

They come in a crowd, armed with weapons. They come as if they will face an army instead of one man. They come as if under their own power. Except that they are but God's means to God's end. That scripture may be fulfilled. That mankind may be reconciled to God. This crowd of soldiers leads Him away. Another crowd, this one including the chief priests, the scribes and the elders, tells lies about Him and bears false witness against Him.

Even so, it takes Jesus to create the circumstances with which they will condemn Him to death. It takes His admission of Truth to move their lies forward.

And, oh, how this incredible irony shakes me to my core. Especially as they humiliate Him, as they shame Him, as the mock Him. Nausea fills my insides as pain fills my heart and tears fill my eyes. Is this really the Jesus I have been following? Is this really the Jesus of miracles, the Jesus of hope, the Jesus of amazing love?

Of course it is.

But to see such anger, such cruelty, such hatred hurled at Him physically hurts me. With each blow, with each ugly action, my muscles tense, my jaw clenches, my hands curl into tightened fists. That such a moment of deep and utter hopelessness will be the birth of hope amazes me. It doesn't seem possible, at least not in this moment of such despair.

And I cannot help but wonder about these men. These men who tonight, in these moments, give in to their basest natures and accost this man, Jesus, in their custody. This man they have seen perform miracles. This man they have heard teach with incredible wisdom. This man they have perhaps even followed at a comfortable distance, perhaps drawn to Him in a way similar to the disciples, perhaps even realizing that there is something about this man that is more than they can understand. And yet tonight they gather around this man, Jesus, and strike Him. Mocking Him. Celebrating their own power.

But what about a few nights from tonight? What then will they feel? What then will they experience? What then will they encounter in their hearts and their souls?

Will they believe the news that this man, Jesus is not in the grave where He was lain?

Will they believe that He was innocent though He hung upon the cross?

Will they believe that He was the fulfillment of the scriptures? That He was the Messiah?

And what if they do?

What if they come to believe His claims about himself and the testimony of His disciples?

What burden will they bear?

Will it be more difficult for them to come before Him then, for them to gather around Him? Will it be more difficult for them to come before the throne of God? Will it be more difficult for them than it will be for me? Or for Peter? Or for any of the disciples who abandoned Him?

We each bear a burden of shame, of guilt, of hurt, don't we? For angry words we speak to someone we love. For lying to someone who trusts us. For hurting someone who cannot defend himself. We each bear a burden of sin.

And that's what this is all about, isn't it?

That's why Jesus went so willingly to the cross as God and as man. Even though the human part of Him begged the Father for some other way, Jesus went willingly. Even when the high priests and scribes and elders and pharisees couldn't trap Him, catch Him, frame Him, He willingly gave them what they needed.

Jesus went willingly.

And He invited us to follow Him and to meet Him there, at the foot of the cross. He invited us.

He invites us still. Daily he invites us to lay down the burdens we bear. Daily he invites us to take on His grace.

Jesus invites us to come to Him even after all that He endured, and after all that we've done, and continue to do. In fact, sometimes, for me, the invitation to His grace comes moment to moment. But the invitation stands.

He invites us to come to Him no matter what. He does not hold our weakness, our striking blows, our ugly, angry actions that we hurl at Him and others against us. That is difficult for my human mind to believe. That is difficult for my human heart to comprehend. That is difficult for my human nature that clings to the smallest wrongs of others against me to fathom.

And yet, I do believe.

I don't comprehend and I cannot fathom, but I *do* believe.

Because I have walked with this man Jesus and I believe He is who He says He is. I believe Him. I believe in Him. I trust Him.

I love Him.

And I can love Him only because He first loved me.

And that is what I am watching as I stand in the shadows of this courtyard, a witness to the end of Jesus' ministry. The end of His life.

I am watching love. Absolute, unconditional, amazing love.

And my heart tells me that though it feels like the end, it is but the beginning.

And I cling to that. I cling to Jesus. Even now as He is mocked and beaten, I cling to Him.

Because He is Jesus.

Because He is I Am.

Because He is love.

Prayer

Dear Jesus, sometimes I project my limited humanity with its messed up, broken and selfish ways onto you. I shrink you down to my limited emotions and understanding. So thank you for allowing me, for *inviting* me, to walk with you on this journey and to witness who you are. Thank you for showing me and reminding me that you are so much more than I can understand and that you are love – pure, absolute, unconditional, amazing love.

Additional Scripture for Reflection

Romans 3:21-26

1 Peter 5:7

Romans 8:38-39

Day 8: The Power of Surrender

Then Jesus went out and made his way, as he customarily did, to the Mount of Olives, and the disciples followed him. When he came to the place, he said to them, "Pray that you will not fall into temptation." He went away from them about a stone's throw, knelt down, and prayed, "Father, if you are willing, take this cup away from me. Yet not my will but yours be done." [Then an angel from heaven appeared to him and strengthened him. And in his anguish he prayed more earnestly, and his sweat was like drops of blood falling to the ground.] When he got up from prayer, he came to the disciples and found them sleeping, exhausted from grief. So he said to them, "Why are you sleeping? Get up and pray that you will not fall into temptation!"

While he was still speaking, suddenly a crowd appeared, and the man named Judas, one of the twelve, was leading them. He walked up to Jesus to kiss him. But Jesus said to him, "Judas, would you betray the Son of Man with a kiss?" When those who were around him saw what was about to happen, they said, "Lord, should we use our swords?" Then one of them struck the high priest's slave, cutting off his right ear. But Jesus said, "Enough of this!" And he touched the man's ear and healed him. Then Jesus said to the chief priests, the officers of the temple guard, and the elders who had come out to get him, "Have you come out with swords and *clubs like you would against an outlaw? Day after day when I was with you in the temple courts, you did not arrest me. But this is your hour, and that of the power of darkness!" **Luke 22:39-53***

There is a beautiful familiarity here on the Mount of Olives. I have learned many things from Jesus and grown closer to Him during the times we spent here this week. I can see why it is a favorite place for Him because of its proximity to Jerusalem and this garden is not far from his friends, Lazarus, Martha, and Mary. But this place that has held a serene and intimate beauty as I've sat with Jesus, has a different feel tonight. It's beauty is cast in shadow and tension; I sense the tension underlying Jesus' words as He tells us to, *"Pray that you may not enter into temptation" (ESV).*

It is not only a warning; it feels more like a prayer. I sense He is concerned as much for us as for Himself right now. Here in the chill of the night, the world has shifted and I feel off balance and unsettled. Something is on the horizon, but it's not until I watch Jesus move away from us and kneel, bowing His head low to the ground, that understanding begins weaving its way into my heart. This is a Jesus I am not used to seeing. Here on this hill underneath a night sky speckled with stars, He is vulnerable. This is Jesus fully human, emotionally naked before His Father, and desperate and afraid.

His prayers include as many groans as words as He pleads with the Father to take away the cup that is His alone to drink. His fully God side comes through in His words of surrender, *"Father, if you are willing, remove this cup from me. Nevertheless, not my*

190

will, but yours be done" (ESV). Beside Jesus, I make out the shape of another, but it is more ethereal than real to me, but I sense a deep love and power hovering over Jesus. God cannot remove the cup from Jesus, but He can strengthen Him in the darkness of this and the coming moments. In response, Jesus' prayers intensify. In fact, they are so much so, the sweat from His brow looks like drops of blood as it falls to the ground. My body is attuned to this place in a whole new way, it's like I can feel the moonlight on my skin and feel the droplets that drip from His brow like the cold, hard ground beneath his knees.

More than anything else, I sense in Him a renewed strength; He is fully man, but also fully God, and it is that God-strength that I feel from Him right now. He knows this is the only way and His Father has done the only thing He can in this moment: given Him the strength He needs to face what is coming. I am not only grateful for this strength for Jesus, but for myself, too.

Too often I have missed out on the strength God provides because I have not sought Him. Unlike Jesus, who though He is God came to this secluded place to seek His Father's strength, I press forward, ever forward, in my own strength. And every time, I stumble, and I fall. I lose hope because I don't seek His face. But tonight, watching Jesus in prayer, I am convicted to make God the focus of my moments — the hours, the minutes, the small increments of my day.

Because while I claim God as the center of my life, it is far too easy to lose that focus in the small moments, the ordinary moments. But if I do not practice seeking Him first in the ordinary moments, it becomes even easier to forget in the extraordinary one. It becomes easier to forget He has promised to be with me in all

191

circumstances, including and especially the ones that feel insurmountable.

There is a verse I hear often and that I repeat just as often: *I can do all things through him who strengthens me (Philippians 4:13 ESV)*. But having watched Jesus here tonight on the Mount of Olives, that verse provides a whole new reality to me. Having witnessed Jesus' human fragility and vulnerability alongside the strengthening from God the Father that renewed this Jesus who is fully human and fully God, I *see* the truth of that verse more clearly, the transformative power of God's strength through our prayers and our complete surrender.

If Jesus made prayer a priority in order to face all the hardship and pain that is coming, what is it that keeps me from doing the same? If Jesus, this man who is fully God, chose to humble Himself here on the cold, hard ground of this garden to seek the Father's face in His vulnerable human fear and emotion, who am I not to do the same? To see God so weak and so strong is a gift I have not appreciated until now, and it is a gift I accept with deep gratitude.

Prayer

Dear Jesus, far too often I choose to push forward on my own and not with You and the Father. Thank for this example showing me the power that comes in surrender. Thank you for surrendering to the Father's will and for taking my place so that I could be forgiven and made new. There is something incredible in Your humanity we witnessed that reminds me there is nothing I go through you don't understand.

Additional Scripture for Reflection

Romans 3:21-26

1 Peter 5:7

Romans 8:38-39

Day 7: In The Shadows of Doubt

After singing a hymn, they went out to the Mount of Olives.

Then Jesus said to them, "This night you will all fall away because of me, for it is written:

'I will strike the shepherd,

and the sheep of the flock will be scattered.'

But after I am raised, I will go ahead of you into Galilee." Peter said to him, "If they all fall away because of you, I will never fall away!" Jesus said to him, "I tell you the truth, on this night, before the rooster crows, you will deny me three times." Peter said to him, "Even if I must die with you, I will never deny you." And all the disciples said the same thing

Now Peter was sitting outside in the courtyard. A slave girl came to him and said, "You also were with Jesus the Galilean." But he denied it in front of them all: "I don't know what you're talking about!" When he went out to the gateway, another slave girl saw him and said to the people there, "This man was with Jesus the Nazarene." He denied it again with an oath, "I do not know the man!" After a little while, those standing there came up to Peter and said, "You really are one of them too – even your accent gives you away!" At that he began to curse, and he swore with an oath, "I do not know the man!" At that moment a rooster crowed. Then Peter remembered what Jesus had said: "Before the rooster crows, you will deny me three times." And he went outside and wept bitterly. **Matthew 26:30-35, 69-75**

As we have traveled these dusty roads together with Jesus, I have developed an affinity for Peter. His impetuous response to Jesus very much matches mine. As soon as we realized it was Jesus approaching the boat during the storm on the Sea of Galilee, I was as eager to step out onto the ocean waves as Peter. When Jesus asked the disciples, *but who do you say that I am*, I was a syllable behind Peter when he immediately replied, "You are the Christ, the Son of the living God" (ESV). And only moments later, when Jesus says He will suffer and die, I share Peter's concern and protectiveness when he rebukes Jesus without hesitation because he does not want to consider losing Jesus who has only just begun His ministry.

Peter's passion for Jesus mirrors my own, and I recognize in him the wonder and excitement to be on this journey with the long-awaited, long-anticipated, and powerfully prophesied Messiah. For generations, families like Peter's have longed for the Messiah's arrival, and, now, at last, He is here and Peter is not only a part of the crowd that follows Him, Peter is one of the Twelve, and, even more, one of Jesus' innermost circle of three.

He loves Jesus so deeply that when Jesus predicts His disciples will all fall away just hours from now, once again Peter is quick to respond, telling Jesus He is wrong. Peter believes even if all the others desert Jesus, he will never abandon his friend. Even when Jesus challenges Peter with the news of how Peter will deny even knowing Jesus before dawn, Peter swears he will die before he denies Jesus.

And that's how it feels in those mountaintop moments with Jesus. When life is going well and our faith is steady and our circumstances require little more from us than the usual daily routine, we are faith-filled and sure-footed, we cannot imagine denying our love for or faith in Jesus. But when we're in the valley? When life feels out of our control and unpredictable and our circumstances are more than we can bear without breaking down, or when we are afraid of what might happen to us or someone we love, faith can become shaky at best.

Even more of a challenge for me is exactly what happens to Peter. Having watched Jesus arrested and taken away, Peter is shaken. As always, in the moment he is the first to draw his sword and defend Jesus. But now that Jesus is gone, the disciples respond just as Jesus foretold — they scatter. Finding himself now alone, Peter follows Jesus at a distance, adrift in the night but vigilantly laying low. Despite his efforts to remain in the shadows, he is called out by a few different people: *This man was with Jesus of Nazareth* and *You're one of them, we can tell by your accent.*

In the shadows, his doubts and fears grow, until, finally Peter panics. Each time he is called out and confronted, instinctively he denies he even knows Jesus. Each time, I cringe. I cringe for Peter, but also for me. Immediately I recall times I have left my faith out of the conversation or remained silent rather than admit I know Jesus or acknowledge I believe He is who He says He is and that I spend my time with Him. Without thinking, I deny Jesus with my silence. Although our denials differ, there is a fear, perhaps even self-preservation, at the core. What might happen if this person learns that I, too, am one of them?

Unfortunately for Peter, his denials are followed by the crow of the rooster announcing the arrival of dawn. And immediately Peter remembers. Immediately he hears Jesus' words echoing through his mind: *Before the rooster crows, you will deny me three times" (ESV)*. And Peter weeps. He weeps because only hours before this moment he vehemently denied he would ever fall away.

As he disappears into the night, I watch him go and my heart aches for him. My own tears stream down my cheeks as once again I recognize myself in him, in his anguish over the loss of Jesus in the Garden of Gethsemane, but even more, the loss of Jesus in denying Him. Even so, I can't help but consider the moment between Jesus and Peter earlier, when Jesus predicted this moment. As is always the case with Jesus, there was no condemnation in Him. In fact, once again, as always, Jesus' eyes held nothing but compassion and love.

And that's what's so amazing, isn't it? Even when we fall short, even when we are less than faithful, even when we deny Him in the ways we do, He still loves us. I want to call out to Peter and remind him of this truth. Beneath my feet, I can still see where Peter's tears hit the ground, the dust dampened by his pain and denial. I stare into the darkness where Peter retreated into the garden where Jesus prayed earlier. I wonder if he is praying now, like Jesus did, or if it's too soon for him still. Maybe he thinks he needs to be alone. Maybe he thinks that's what he deserves because of what he's done.

But that's not how Jesus deals with us and I want to remind Peter of that truth. It's a truth I know he knows after spending the past three years with Jesus, watching how He dealt with people. Jesus never deals harshly with us, no matter what we've done or how awful the thing we think we've done. If we turn back to Him, He is there. If we repent for our mistakes, even something as big as denying Him, He will forgive us. He will never stop loving us. Peter, I whisper into the darkness, He still loves you. Remember that, my friend. He still loves you and that's what He's about to prove. To you and to me.

Prayer

Dear Jesus, You know all too well how often I deny You and let my fears or my desire to fit in and be accepted by the world influence my words as well as my deeds. But You are always willing to forgive me when I turn back to You. And You remind me that in those moments of panic, when I think it will be easier to deny You, if I pray, You will be my strength. Help me not to give in to the shadows of doubt, but to step into the Light of faith and truth.

Additional Scripture for Reflection

Psalm 23

John 10:1-18

John 21:15-19

A Day of Reading and Reflection

Scripture for Reflection:

John 12:27-43

"Now my soul is greatly distressed. And what should I say? 'Father, deliver me from this hour'? No, but for this very reason I have come to this hour. Father, glorify your name." Then a voice came from heaven, "I have glorified it, and I will glorify it again." The crowd that stood there and heard the voice said that it had thundered. Others said that an angel had spoken to him. Jesus said, "This voice has not come for my benefit but for yours. Now is the judgment of this world; now the ruler of this world will be driven out. And I, when I am lifted up from the earth, will draw all people to myself." (Now he said this to indicate clearly what kind of death he was going to die.)

Then the crowd responded, "We have heard from the law that the Christ will remain forever. How can you say, 'The Son of Man must be lifted up'? Who is this Son of Man?" Jesus replied, "The light is with you for a little while longer. Walk while you have the light, so that the darkness may not overtake you. The one who walks in the darkness does not know where he is going. While you have the light, believe in the light, so that you may become sons of light." When Jesus had said these things, he went away and hid himself from them.

Although Jesus had performed so many miraculous signs before them, they still refused to believe in him, so that the word of Isaiah the prophet would be fulfilled. He said, **"Lord, who has believed our message, and to whom has the arm of the Lord been revealed?"** *For this reason they could not believe, because again Isaiah said,*

> **"He has blinded their eyes**
> **and hardened their heart,**
> **so that they would not see with their eyes**
> **and understand with their heart,**
> **and turn to me, and I would heal them."**

Isaiah said these things because he saw Christ's glory, and spoke about him.

Nevertheless, even among the rulers many believed in him, but because of the Pharisees they would not confess Jesus to be the Christ, so that they would not be put out of the synagogue. For they loved praise from men more than praise from God.

Isaiah 6:1-10

In the year of King Uzziah's death, I saw the sovereign master seated on a high, elevated throne. The hem of his robe filled the temple. Seraphs stood over him; each one had six wings. With two wings they covered their faces, with two they covered their feet, and they used the remaining two to fly. They called out to one another, "Holy, holy, holy is the Lord who commands armies! His majestic splendor fills the entire earth!" The sound of their voices shook the door frames, and the temple was filled with smoke.

I said, "Too bad for me! I am destroyed, for my lips are contaminated by sin, and I live among people whose lips are contaminated by sin. My eyes have seen the king, the Lord who commands armies." But then one of the seraphs flew toward me. In his hand was a hot coal he had taken from the altar with tongs. He touched my mouth with it and said, "Look, this coal has touched your lips. Your evil is removed; your sin is forgive." I heard the voice of the sovereign master say, "Whom will I send? Who will go on our behalf?" I answered, "Here I am, send me!" He said, "Go and tell these people:

> *'Listen continually, but don't understand!*
> *Look continually, but don't perceive!'*

Make the hearts of these people calloused;
> *make their ears deaf and their eyes blind!*
> *Otherwise they might see with their eyes and hear with their ears,*
> *their hearts might understand and they might repent and be healed."*

Acts 3:11-26

While the man was hanging on to Peter and John, all the people, completely astounded, ran together to them in the covered walkway called Solomon's Portico. When Peter saw this, he declared to the people, "Men of Israel, why are you amazed at this? Why do you stare at us as if we had made this man walk by our own power or piety? The God of Abraham, Isaac, and Jacob, the God of our forefathers, has glorified his servant Jesus, whom you handed over and rejected in the presence of Pilate after he had decided to release him. But you rejected the Holy and Righteous One and asked that a man who was a murderer be released to you. You killed the Originator of life, whom God raised from the dead. To this fact we are witnesses! And on the basis of faith in Jesus' name, his very name has made this man – whom you see and know – strong. The faith that is through Jesus has given him this complete health in the presence of you all. And now, brothers, I know you acted in ignorance, as your rulers did too. But the things God foretold long ago through all the prophets – that his Christ would suffer – he has fulfilled in this way. Therefore repent and turn back so that your sins may be wiped out, so that times of refreshing may come from the presence of the Lord, and so that he may send the Messiah appointed for you – that is, Jesus. This one heaven must receive until the time all things are restored, which God declared from times long ago through his holy prophets. Moses said, 'The Lord your God will raise up for you a prophet like me from among your brothers. You must obey him in everything he tells you. Every person who does not obey that prophet will be destroyed and thus removed from the people.' And all the prophets, from Samuel and those who followed him, have spoken about and announced these days. You are the sons of the prophets and of the covenant that God made with your ancestors, saying to Abraham, 'And in your descendants all the nations of the earth will be blessed.' God raised up his servant and sent him first to you, to bless you by turning each one of you from your iniquities."

Psalm 85

For the music director; written by the Korahites, a psalm.

O Lord, you showed favor to your land;
you restored the well-being of Jacob.

You pardoned the wrongdoing of your people;
you forgave all their sin. (Selah)

You withdrew all your fury;
you turned back from your raging anger.

Restore us, O God our deliverer!
Do not be dispelled with us!

Will you stay mad at us forever?
Will you remain angry throughout future generations?

Will you not revive us once more?
Then your people will rejoice in you!

O Lord, show us your loyal love!
Bestow on us your deliverance!

I will listen to what God the Lord says.
For he will make peace with his people, his faithful followers.
Yet they must not return to their foolish ways.

Certainly his loyal rollers will soon experience his deliverance;

then his spender will again appear in our land.

Loyal love and faithfulness meet;
deliverance and peace greet each other with a
kiss.

Faithfulness grows from the ground,
and deliverance looks down from the sky.

Yes the Lord will bestow his good blessings,
and our land will yield its crops.

Deliverance goes before him,
and prepares a pathway for him.

Day 6: Finding Little Satisfaction

Early in the morning, after forming a plan, the chief priests with the elders and the experts in the law and the whole Sanhedrin tied Jesus up, led him away, and handed him over to Pilate. So Pilate asked him, "Are you the king of the Jews?" He replied, "You say so." Then the chief priests began to accuse him repeatedly. So Pilate asked him again, "Have you nothing to say? See how many charges they are bringing against you!" But Jesus made no further reply, so that Pilate was amazed.

During the feast it was customary to release one prisoner to the people, whomever they requested. A man named Barabbas was imprisoned with rebels who had committed murder during an insurrection. Then the crowd came up and began to ask Pilate to release a prisoner for them, as was his custom. So Pilate asked them, "Do you want me to release the king of the Jews for you?" (For he knew that the chief priests had handed him over because of envy.) But the chief priests stirred up the crowd to have him release Barabbas instead. So Pilate spoke to them again, "Then what do you want me to do with the one you call king of the Jews?" They shouted back, "Crucify him!" Pilate asked them, "Why? What has he done wrong?" But they shouted more insistently, "Crucify him!" Because he wanted to satisfy the crowd, Pilate released Barabbas for them. Then, after he had Jesus flogged, he handed him over to be crucified. **Mark 15:1-15**

He may be the Roman prefect, but Pontius Pilate has little power over what the chief priests are trying to create. By the look on Pilate's face, the magnitude of what's happening before him is not lost. Even so, there is something more in his eyes, something that indicates he would rather be anywhere else than here having take care of a problem that is not his to worry about. Pilate chooses to play along, and it seems he is hoping the man bound before him will save him from having to do the hard work set before him. Alas, that is not what Jesus does. Rather than confirm the charges when Pilate asks Him if He is indeed King of the Jews, Jesus offers only a simple statement, *"You have said so" (ESV).* They are the only words He says and His silence leaves Pilate in awe. But Jesus' silence also leave Pilate with little wiggle room as the prefect set in place to dole out Roman rule in this dusty town.

Since Jesus refuses to relieve Pilate of the duty set before him, Pilate hopes to get the crowd to do it. As is the tradition, he offers to free a prisoner, and he appears confident the crowd certainly will choose Jesus. He has heard the stories of Jesus and how the crowd follows Him. Even when the crowd chooses Barabbas, Pilate can't help but try again. He knows this is playing out because of the jealousy harbored by the Pharisees and chief priests. Surely the people know it, too. Certainly they realize Jesus is not guilty. But when he presents Jesus to the crowd for release, the crowd responds with cries to crucify Him.

At this point, Pilate seems rattled by the ferocity of the crowd and their demand to put Jesus to death. Whatever else Pilate might have hoped to accomplish here this morning, he is left with

Jesus still bound before him and a crowd that is growing into an angry mob. Rather than stir up the crowd further, he acquiesces to the crowd, releasing the murderous Barabbas, beating Jesus, and turning Him over to be crucified.

I stand in disbelief.

Just like that, Jesus path has come to an end; He is condemned to crucifixion because Pilate relented to the crowd's demands. My head spins with what is happening. Pilate chooses to satisfy the crowd, and the crowd? They were stirred up by the Pharisees. As for the Pharisees, their sole motivation is envy and self-preservation of their role and status. Surely Pilate knows this. Surely he understands what's happening here.

So, why does he do it?

Initially I am tempted to yell, to call Pilate out for his cowardice. That this man in power so easily gives in to the crowd before him deeply angers me. But as the crowd begins to disperse and Pilate disappears into his personal sanctuary, the truth of what's happened here seeps into my thoughts. Pilate did what he did to placate the crowd. When faced with a crowd's opposing ideas and desires, Pilate did what many of us tend to do: he took the easy way out.

Wishing to satisfy the crowd.

How often do we, as Christ's followers, do this, too? How often have I done this? How often have I made small attempts to make a point or demonstrate integrity and make the right choice, only to falter in the face of peer pressure or popular opinion?

Wishing to satisfy the crowd.

Pilate released Barabbas even though he recognized the rulers were jealous of who Jesus was. He knew the right thing to do and he even seemed to want to do the right thing. But when it came down to doing the right thing, his fear, or perhaps his pride, didn't allow him to. I know that feeling. I know that underlying desire to not cause upset, to keep the peace. And the irony is that almost always in those moments, I lose *my* peace. Within me, the turmoil of wanting to do what's right versus wanting to satisfy the crowd is difficult to navigate.

Wishing to satisfy the crowd.

And what of the crowd, asking for the worst criminal rather than choosing Jesus? Isn't that how it happens sometimes? There are those we look up to, those who are where we want to be or who we thought we wanted to be like, and they're telling us we don't want Jesus, we want Barabbas. We know it's not true, but we're not sure we want to be the single voice calling out for Jesus when everyone else is choosing Barabbas.

Wishing to satisfy the crowd.

Haven't we all, at some point in our lives, made similar, reckless choices? Watching Jesus being led away to be crucified, I want to run after Him and tell Him I'm sorry for the times when I should have chosen Him and didn't. He looks at me over His shoulder, and the truth, His Truth, washes over me. He already knows, and He's about to do the only thing that will make up for those moments and many more.

He's about to die for me.

Prayer

Dear Jesus, I confess to you that there are times even now when I look to the crowd, I look to them for my worth or I look to be accepted by the world. I hear Your Truth, and yet the immediacy of the here and now pulls me away from You. If I don't spend time with you each day, it's much too easy for me to be lured by the things of this world. Forgive me when I ignore Your Truth, I pray, and restore my desire for You, that I might seek you and live my life for you boldly.

Additional Scripture for Reflection

1 Timothy 1:6-14

Philippians 3:12-21

Matthew 6:19-24

Day 5: The Absolute Truth of Jesus

While this was happening, the high priest questioned Jesus about his disciples and about his teaching. Jesus replied, "I have spoken publicly to the world. I always taught in the synagogues and in the temple courts, where all the Jewish people assemble together. I have said nothing in secret. Why do you ask me? Ask those who heard what I said. They know what I said." When Jesus had said this, one of the high priest's officers who stood nearby struck him on the face and said, "Is that the way you answer the high priest?" Jesus replied, "If I have said something wrong, confirm what is wrong. But if I spoke correctly, why strike me?" Then Annas sent him, still tied up, to Caiaphas the high priest.

Meanwhile Simon Peter was standing in the courtyard warming himself. They said to him, "You aren't one of his disciples too, are you?" Peter denied it: "I am not!" One of the high priest's slaves, a relative of the man whose ear Peter had cut off, said, "Did I not see you in the orchard with him?" Then Peter denied it again, and immediately a rooster crowed.

Then they brought Jesus from Caiaphas to the Roman governor's residence. (Now it was very early morning.) They did not go into the governor's residence so they would not be ceremonially defiled, but could eat the Passover meal. So Pilate came outside to them and said, *"What accusation do you bring against this man?"* They replied, *"If this man were not a criminal, we would not have handed him over to you."*

Pilate told them, *"Take him yourselves and pass judgment on him according to your own law!"* The Jewish leaders replied, *"We cannot legally put anyone to death."* (This happened to fulfill the word Jesus had spoken when he indicated what kind of death he was going to die.)

So Pilate went back into the governor's residence, summoned Jesus, and asked him, *"Are you the king of the Jews?"* Jesus replied, *"Are you saying this on your own initiative, or have others told you about me?"* Pilate answered, *"I am not a Jew, am I? Your own people and your chief priests handed you over to me. What have you done?"*

Jesus replied, *"My kingdom is not from this world. If my kingdom were from this world, my servants would be fighting to keep me from being handed over to the Jewish authorities. But as it is, my kingdom is not from here."* Then Pilate said, *"So you are a king!"* Jesus replied, *"You say that I am a king. For this reason I was born, and for this reason I came into the world – to testify to the truth. Everyone who belongs to the truth listens to my voice."* Pilate asked, *"What is truth?"*

When he had said this he went back outside to the Jewish leaders and announced, *"I find no basis for an accusation against him. But it is your custom that I release one prisoner for you at the Passover. So do you want me to release for you the king of the Jews?" Then they shouted back, "Not this man, but Barabbas!" (Now Barabbas was a revolutionary.)* ***John 18:19-40***

What is it about Jesus? Have you ever wondered what it was about Him that drew people to Him and made His disciples drop what it was they were doing and follow Him? No questions asked, people just up and followed this man, drew near to this man, trusted this man.

So, then what was it about Jesus that rattled the Pharisees and the scribes and the elders? Did they see in Jesus what the disciples saw in Him? Or were they too blinded by their need for power and the comfort of the status quo? Whatever their blindness, they have finally claimed the victory they have so desperately sought and for which they have plotted so ruthlessly: Jesus is in custody and has been sent to Pilate.

Jesus' demise is imminent.

And yet, Pilate is not so easily sold on the bill of goods he is given, that Jesus is doing evil. Even after questioning Jesus directly, he is not convinced that there is anything worthy of which to convict this man. Although Pilate does not seem to understand everything that Jesus tells him, he does seem to see something in Jesus. Perhaps he sees the same thing in Jesus that the disciples saw.

The one thing that is clear is that Pilate is drawn to Jesus' reference to truth, to *the* Truth.

What is truth? This seems to be the point that resonates deepest with Pilate. Jesus tells him that He has come into the world to bear witness to the truth and those who are of the truth listen to His voice.

The Truth.

It's pretty incredible to me, watching from the shadows, the levels of truth, the roots of relativism, that are so obvious here, in Jesus' day. What the Pharisees claim as truth, the essence of Jesus as the Truth, the need of Pilate to know and to understand truth.

What is truth?

Have you ever found yourself asking this question? It seems obvious to you when you are alone, when you are studying scripture and looking at how it applies to your life. Perhaps you have no misgivings about the idea of absolute truth when you are in the presence of Jesus, like the disciples, or like Pilate. But then, when you are in the world, when you mix with friends or co-workers or even family, the question of truth, of what is truth, slowly creeps into your thoughts. People suggest, "Well, that is true for you," or, "Well, there really is no such thing as absolutes or absolute truth." But, isn't there?

Isn't that what Jesus was? The way and the truth and the life. Isn't that what Jesus is? And isn't that what Jesus tells Pilate in their brief exchange? Those simple words seem to be enough to rattle Pilate. When he looks at Jesus, when he listens to Jesus, he does not see and he does not hear what the Pharisees do. He sees and hears what the disciples saw and heard - he sees and hears the Truth and he wants more of it. He wants to understand it. Perhaps he even wants to apply it in the very moment he shares with Jesus as Jesus stands before him, convicted by the Pharisees.

But truth seems to be a cunning concept, almost elusive at times, as we see with Pilate's attempts to right what he sees as an obvious wrong. *I find no guilt in Him.*

But like the crowd of soldiers who arrested Jesus in the garden, Pilate is merely one of God's means to God's end. Pilate's efforts, although admirable, would only be successful if God deemed it so.

"I find no guilt in Him," Pilate announces to the crowd, and so he offers willingly to release Jesus, this King of the Jews, to them. But they refuse His offer. They refuse Jesus. They refuse the Truth.

Instead of truth, they request a common criminal, a thief, a liar.

Have you ever refused the Truth in exchange for lies, or power, or personal gain, or instant gratification? Have you ever stood with the crowd, blended in with the crowd, and chosen the easier side instead of standing up, standing out, for the Truth?

I wish I could say that I have not. I wish I could tell you that whenever I am presented with a choice, I stand up for the Truth and refuse to muddle it with the gray of doubt, or fear, or weakness. But that isn't true. Too often I waffle, especially on difficult issues that stir up strong emotions in so many. Rather than speak truth, rather than represent the Truth, I fade into the background and cry out for Barabbas. I cry out for the easier option.

Fortunately, the Truth wins in the end. Whether we choose it, whether we defend it, whether we stand up for it, the Truth wins. How freeing to know that Jesus isn't depending on me for the victory. How freeing to know that Jesus, who was the way, the truth and the life, defeats all of their lies, all of their manipulation, all of their shame and sets me free in the process.

And, so, by His death, I am released from the crowd, no longer just an anonymous sinner who cries out for Barabbas, but one person, one child of the Father, who has been redeemed and who will heed Jesus' invitation to follow Him, to know Him, to trust Him. And this gives me the freedom and the boldness to shine a light for truth and for love in a world that too often fails to believe in either.

Because despite the ideals of relativism, absolutes exist: absolute truth and absolute love. And they both exist in this man standing before Pilate.

They both exist in this man, this Savior, this Rescuing Redeemer called Jesus.

Prayer

Dear Jesus, thank you for your Truth and for the abundant life that you offer me because you are the way, the truth and the life. Thank you for the freedom that comes with your absolute love and your absolute truth, and forgive me when I hide my light and deny your truth. Thank you for being the One to reconcile me to the Father and for redeeming my mistakes or the choices that harm me in order to serve your good and holy purpose.

Additional Scripture for Reflection

Romans 8:28-30

Genesis 50:15-21

John 14:1-7

Day 4: The Fault Line of Blame

Then Pilate took Jesus and had him flogged severely. The soldiers braided a crown of thorns and put it on his head, and they clothed him in a purple robe. They came up to him again and again and said, "Hail, king of the Jews!" And they struck him repeatedly in the face.

Again Pilate went out and said to the Jewish leaders, "Look, I am bringing him out to you, so that you may know that I find no reason for an accusation against him." So Jesus came outside, wearing the crown of thorns and the purple robe. Pilate said to them, "Look, here is the man!" When the chief priests and their officers saw him, they shouted out, "Crucify him! Crucify him!" Pilate said, "You take him and crucify him! Certainly I find no reason for an accusation against him!" The Jewish leaders replied, "We have a law, and according to our law he ought to die, because he claimed to be the Son of God!"

When Pilate heard what they said, he was more afraid than ever, and he went back into the governor's residence and said to Jesus, "Where do you come from?" But Jesus gave him no answer. So Pilate said, "Do you refuse to speak to me? Don't you know I have the authority to release you, and to crucify you?" Jesus replied, "You would have no authority over me at all, unless it was given to you from above. Therefore the one who handed me over to you is guilty of greater sin."

From this point on, Pilate tried to release him. But the Jewish leaders shouted out, "If you release this man, you are no friend of Caesar! Everyone who claims to be a king opposes Caesar!" When Pilate heard these words he brought Jesus outside and sat down on the judgment seat in the place called "The Stone Pavement" (Gabbatha in Aramaic). (Now it was the day of preparation for the Passover, about noon.) Pilate said to the Jewish leaders, "Look, here is your king!"

Then they shouted out, "Away with him! Away with him! Crucify him!" Pilate asked, "Shall I crucify your king?" The high priests replied, "We have no king except Caesar!" Then Pilate handed him over to them to be crucified. **John 19:1-16**

Certainly I find no reason for an accusation against him! Or, as a different translation says, *For I find no guilt in Him (ESV).*

With these words, Pilate manages to sum up the entire birth, life, ministry, impending death and eventual resurrection of Jesus. Jesus' whole reason for leaving His heavenly throne and descending to earth, for being born as a babe in Bethlehem 33 years prior to this moment, was to be the unblemished lamb; the final sacrifice. Even so, these final hours are difficult to witness.

There is no guilt, no sin in Him, but He is flogged.

There is no guilt, no sin in Him, but He is mocked.

There is no guilt, no sin in Him, but He is rejected.

There is no guilt, no sin in Him, but He is humiliated.

There is no guilt, no sin in Him, but He is given a crown of thorns.

There is no guilt, no sin in Him, but He is declared guilty.

Jesus is God, but He is also human. He is a man who in these moments feels the same emotions we experience in our lives. And having walked with Him on the journey to Jerusalem, His passion and His purpose and His incredible sacrifice take on a deeper, heart-piercing perspective. The pain He endures and the heartbreak He experiences are beyond my comprehension.

There is no guilt, no sin in Him, but me? I am guilty on a regular basis throughout each day. Repeatedly I hang my head and acknowledge my words spoken in anger or my lack of gratitude or my selfishness or my litany of any number of shortfalls and seek His forgiveness. All of these shortfalls are part of the very reason that I stand here in Jerusalem and watch as Jesus is flogged and crowned with thorns and mocked. I watch as He is stripped of His clothes as well as His dignity and is exposed in all of His humanness and vulnerability.

Who is to blame for Jesus' death? There is a long line of those at fault and it starts with me. Because other than me and you and every person who was ever born or will be born, including Pilate, the Pharisees, Judas, the only One responsible for Jesus' death is God. And Jesus. And the Holy Spirit. The Trinity. Before the world was created, before Adam and Eve, before the snake in the Garden of Eden, the plan was put in place that Jesus would die.

Because we would need Him to. Because God knew, the Trinity knew, the only way to repair the relationship broken in the Garden was by God's own hands. And the only way to do that was through God himself, in the form of Jesus Christ, fully God and fully man, sacrificed once for all.

Did Pontius Pilate sentence Jesus to death? Yes, but not without the authority of God.

Did the Pharisees and Sadducees and elders and scribes bear false witness and manufacture the circumstances of Jesus' arrest? Yes, but not without the authority of God.

Did Judas betray Jesus with a kiss in the very garden where He often met with Jesus and the disciples to pray and enjoy intimate fellowship? Yes, but not without the authority of God.

Jesus knows me and yet He loves me anyway and He chose to die so that I might know Him, too. The question of who in all of these circumstances and moments was responsible for the death of Jesus in whom Pilate found no guilt is but a formality. The more important fact is that Jesus died and He did so willingly, as part of God's plan to rescue His people from darkness and from sin and from hopelessness.

But as I watch Jesus and as I listen to the voices of the angry crowd shouting for His death, I cannot help but count myself guilty. Maybe it's because it hurts too much to watch my Savior endure so much suffering in my place. Because that's what it comes down to.

It should have been me. It should have been you. It should have been the Pharisees, the Sadducees, the disciples, the Roman soldiers, the angry mob, Pilate. It should have been all of us but instead it was only Jesus.

Only Jesus could take on the enemy and win.

Only Jesus could defeat death.

Only Jesus could pay so high a ransom.

Only Jesus could withstand the judgment of and separation from God that was required.

Only Jesus could redeem us and reconcile us to God.

Only Jesus could love with such an amazing, unconditional, sacrificial love.

Only Jesus.

Prayer

Dear Jesus, when I stop and consider what you did that day on the cross, I can barely breathe. Forgive me when I live my life with a sense of entitlement instead of the sense of gratitude and humility that points others to you. Thank you for being the Hero of my story, the One who stepped in to take my judgment and my punishment. I pray, Lord, that my words and my heart will bring you glory today. May your name be praised.

Additional Scripture for Reflection

Hebrews 9:18-28

Hebrews 10:1-10

Romans 5:6-17

Day 3: Once {and} for All

Then the governor's soldiers took Jesus into the governor's residence and gathered the whole cohort around him. They stripped him and put a scarlet robe around him, and after braiding a crown of thorns, they put it on his head. They put a staff in his right hand, and kneeling down before him, they mocked him: "Hail, king of the Jews!" They spat on him and took the staff and struck him repeatedly on the head. When they had mocked him, they stripped him of the robe and put his own clothes back on him. Then they led him away to crucify him.

As they were going out, they found a man from Cyrene named Simon, whom they forced to carry his cross. They came to a place called Golgotha (which means "Place of the Skull") and offered Jesus wine mixed with gall to drink. But after tasting it, he would not drink it. When they had crucified him, they divided his clothes by throwing dice. Then they sat down and kept guard over him there. Above his head they put the charge against him, which read: "This is Jesus, the king of the Jews." Then two outlaws were crucified with him, one on his right and one on his left. Those who passed by defamed him, shaking their heads and saying, "You who can destroy the temple and rebuild it in three days, save yourself! If you are God's Son, come down from the cross!" In the same way even the chief priests – together with the experts in the law and elders – were mocking him: "He saved others, but he cannot save himself! He is the king of Israel! If he comes down now from the cross, we will believe in him! He trusts in God – let God, if he wants to, deliver him now because he said, 'I am God's Son'!" The robbers who were crucified with him also spoke abusively to him. **Matthew 27:27-44**

The Gospel stories recounting the final hours of Jesus' life are as familiar to me as the Gospel stories of His birth. I have read them, I have heard them, I have listened to sermons about them and even have watched them in the Mel Gibson movie, *The Passion of the Christ.* But the thing about all of those experiences is that they are brief and therefore they do not require much of me. They do not tax my emotions or my heart more than I think I can bear.

Even as intense and visually visceral as *The Passion of the Christ* scenes were, even as much as they placed me into those moments with Jesus, I was still able to distance myself through the shared experience of a full theater and cathartic conversations after the film.

However, this journey with Jesus to Jerusalem removes those barriers. It is me and Jesus and I am immersed in the moments with Him, not merely touched by them; I do not simply brush up against them, I experience them in all of their pain and horror and repulsion. Just as there is no escape for Jesus, because He willingly drinks this cup, I choose not to escape but to be a willing witness to these events so that I may be changed. *Truly changed.*

So, I crouch in the shadows with my fists clenched as tightly as my jaw and fight the urge to flee, to fight and to weep simultaneously. His flesh is bleeding and mutilated from the scourging, His face is grossly swollen from countless blows, and His pain is palpable even from this distance. But that is not the end of His suffering, of this bitter cup from which He so willingly drinks tonight.

Heaping more shame and humiliation upon His already hurting and vulnerable human heart, the soldiers call in the whole battalion, a number that likely equals almost 500 men, as they strip Him of His clothes and His dignity and His deity. They mock Him and spit on Him and strike Him. They twist a crown from thorns and press it onto His head, the nail-sized, razor-like thorns cutting into His tender flesh.

This man is not just an ordinary man. This man is not just another criminal. This is Jesus. This is God. He is the Savior who will sacrifice himself for each of these men as much as for the disciples He loves. But these men don't know that. Maybe they never will. And none of that matters to Jesus, because *His sacrifice is once for all*.

This is the what Jesus came to do, what He came to endure. He came to endure all of the anger, hatred and rejection from man and to bear all of the wrath of God. He came to be despised, He came to suffer and He came to be slain. The sacrificial lamb for the atonement of sin.

That is why, after they have beaten Him, bloodied Him, mocked Him, humiliated Him, and brought Him as low as they can, when the guards offer Him the wine mixed with gall, He tastes it and refuses it. He recognizes the narcotic mixture intended to dull the pain of the spikes that will be driven into His hands and into His feet.

He came to endure *all* of the pain, to bear the *whole* burden, to drink *to the dregs* this bitter cup of crucifixion.

And as He is raised up on the cross like the serpent on the pole, He faces the last and worst moment of His mission: the agonizing separation from the Father, *His Father.* Those elders, scribes and chief priests who have gathered at Golgotha continue to hurl insults at Him. Random passersby deride Him. Even the criminals who hang on either side of Him mock and revile Him. All to little consequence or effect at this point.

Because nothing will match the anguish He will experience when God the Father abandons Him to death, forsaking His only Son for the sake of mankind. For the sake of me, and for the sake of you, and for the sake of those who came before us and those who will come after us. *Once for all.*

The shadow of the cross looms large before me as I huddle with Peter, James and John and others who have gathered here to watch and to weep and to wait. For the end is upon us but the minutes tick by slowly, each one bringing excruciation, fear, tears.

I lift my eyes to the cross and I cannot help but wonder, *how is it, Jesus, that you would take my place?*

How is it that you would die for me?

Prayer

Dear Jesus, I cannot truly understand completely the magnitude of all of this suffering. I am barely able to absorb what you endured at the hands of these cruel and brutal soldiers and the religious leaders. And I am humbled, so incredibly humbled, because it is my sin, too, that placed this bitter cup in your hand. I am guilty where you were not. And so I am overwhelmed by your extravagant expression of love that you would die for me. That you would give me life through your grace and your death. So that I might live, and not just live but thrive, live abundantly *with* you. How awesome you are my Lord and my Savior.

Additional Scripture for Reflection

Isaiah 53:3-6

Romans 6:1-11

Hebrews 1

Day 2: Good Friday: Sacred Chaos

Then Pilate handed him over to them to be crucified.

So they took Jesus, and carrying his own cross he went out to the place called "The Place of the Skull" (called in Aramaic Golgotha). There they crucified him along with two others, one on each side, with Jesus in the middle. Pilate also had a notice written and fastened to the cross, which read: "Jesus the Nazarene, the king of the Jews." Thus many of the Jewish residents of Jerusalem read this notice, because the place where Jesus was crucified was near the city, and the notice was written in Aramaic, Latin, and Greek. Then the chief priests of the Jews said to Pilate, "Do not write, 'The king of the Jews,' but rather, 'This man said, I am king of the Jews.'" Pilate answered, "What I have written, I have written."

*Now when the soldiers crucified Jesus, they took his clothes and made four shares, one for each soldier, and the tunic remained. (Now the tunic was seamless, woven from top to bottom as a single piece.) So the soldiers said to one another, "Let's not tear it, but throw dice to see who will get it." This took place to fulfill the scripture that says, "**They divided my garments among them, and for my clothing they threw dice**." So the soldiers did these things.*

Now standing beside Jesus' cross were his mother, his mother's sister, Mary the wife of Clopas, and Mary Magdalene. So when Jesus saw his mother and the disciple whom he loved standing there, he said to his mother, "Woman, look, here is your son!" He then said to his disciple, "Look, here is your mother!" From that very time the disciple took her into his own home.

After this Jesus, realizing that by this time everything was completed, said (in order to fulfill the scripture), "I am thirsty!" A jar full of sour wine was there, so they put a sponge soaked in sour wine on a branch of hyssop and lifted it to his mouth. When he had received the sour wine, Jesus said, "It is completed!" Then he bowed his head and gave up his spirit.

*Then, because it was the day of preparation, so that the bodies should not stay on the crosses on the Sabbath (for that Sabbath was an especially important one), the Jewish leaders asked Pilate to have the victims' legs broken and the bodies taken down. So the soldiers came and broke the legs of the two men who had been crucified with Jesus, first the one and then the other. But when they came to Jesus and saw that he was already dead, they did not break his legs. But one of the soldiers pierced his side with a spear, and blood and water flowed out immediately. And the person who saw it has testified (and his testimony is true, and he knows that he is telling the truth), so that you also may believe. For these things happened so that the scripture would be fulfilled, "**Not a bone of his will be broken**." And again another scripture* *says, "**They will look on the one whom they have pierced.**"*

After this, Joseph of Arimathea, a disciple of Jesus (but secretly, because he feared the Jewish leaders), asked Pilate if he could remove the body of Jesus. Pilate gave him permission, so he went and took the body away. Nicodemus, the man who had previously come to Jesus at night, accompanied Joseph, carrying a mixture of myrrh and aloes weighing about seventy-five pounds. Then they took Jesus' body and wrapped it, with the aromatic spices, in strips of linen cloth according to Jewish burial customs. Now at the place where Jesus was crucified there was a garden, and in the garden was a new tomb where no one had yet been buried. And so, because it was the Jewish day of preparation and the tomb was nearby, they placed Jesus' body there. **John 19:16-42**

It is finished.

They have crucified my King and He hangs lifeless on the cross and the darkness deepens around me.

Even though I stand with His disciples, His mother, and His other followers, I am alone, alone in my despair, alone in my grief, and alone in my fear.

In this moment, they have won.

In this moment, they have stopped Him and saved themselves from His convicting, piercing words.

In this moment, they have pierced His hands, His feet, His side.

In this moment, they have convicted Him although there was no guilt or sin in Him.

Darkness settles thicker upon my heart as the heavens pour out darkness and rain, surrounding the cross and the crowd and me in its storm and its grief.

As Joseph of Arimathea and Nicodemus anoint His body, wrap Him in linens and lay Him in the tomb, I am struck by the eerie similarity of this image to the night of His birth, when He was anointed with life through Mary, wrapped in swaddling clothes and laid in the manger and my heart breaks a little more.

As the rain pours down and the crowd disperses each to his own home, I wind my way back to the Garden of Gethsemane, the most sacred place I can think of going so that I can reflect on my time with Jesus, my time spent at His dusty feet during this Jerusalem journey.

I stand in the spot where He prayed so often, pouring out His heart to His Father. I wander through the darkened places, find a rock, and lower myself to the ground, back against the hardness of the stone. Here, in this garden, His garden, really, with the earth beneath me, I feel connected to Him again and I trace my fingers along the dusty ground. I can almost feel Him here. I move to my knees, close my eyes, and hold out my heart to Jesus.

Like the heavens pour down its rains, I pour out my gratitude, my adoration, my love, my limited, too-often-conditional, extremely fragile, all-too-human love. But it is all that I have, as fallible as it is, and so it is what I offer Him.

And that's when it happens -- the uncontrollable, body-wracking sobs that shake all of me, deep down to my heart.

He is gone. It is finished. His dusty feet will not walk these roads again. He will not teach in the synagog again. He will not break bread with His disciples again.

In this moment there is only brokenness, darkness, deep, piercing sadness and loneliness. My body shakes violently as the sobs continue and I long with an aching in my soul for just one more moment with Jesus on this side of heaven. I yearn for one more moment in His presence so I can hear His voice and listen to His words and look into His eyes and be seen as I am.

And what if I missed something He told me? How will I remember all the stories He shared or the lessons He taught. What if I can't recall all those parables? What do I do now? Where can I go? How can I possibly go back to my life as it was before taking this walk with Him and sitting at His dusty feet?

I yearn for one more moment so I can see His smile, hear His laugh, and watch His love.

His love.

His love is why I sit here alone in this garden. Because of His love. His extravagant, sacrificial, unconditional, amazing, all-encompassing love.

And my heart yearns for that love more than anything right now.

But I realize that love is being poured out over me in these moments, in this garden, in this rain. His love is being wrapped around me even in my sadness. It is being freely given.

It is being freely - even greedily - received.

Prayer

Dear Jesus, your death leaves me speechless. Breathless. Though I know that you have given up your life willingly, I've seen you struggle with this moment as you prayed in the garden. And I watched the humiliation and suffering you endured even to get to this place, here, on the cross. Oh, Jesus, how can I get so caught up in the things of this world so easily, forgetting what you did for me on the cross? Living like it doesn't matter as much as it does? Forgive me, Jesus, when I live as if your sacrifice was less than everything. And thank you, Lord, for inviting me to walk with you to this time and place and for inviting me back whenever I wander off from this, my true home: with you.

Additional Scripture for Reflection

Psalm 30

Jeremiah 31:9-14

Psalm 22

Day 1: Saturday — The In-Between

Now when it was evening, there came a rich man from Arimathea, named Joseph, who was also a disciple of Jesus. He went to Pilate and asked for the body of Jesus. Then Pilate ordered that it be given to him. Joseph took the body, wrapped it in a clean linen cloth, and placed it in his own new tomb that he had cut in the rock. Then he rolled a great stone across the entrance of the tomb and went away. (Now Mary Magdalene and the other Mary were sitting there, opposite the tomb.)

The next day (which is after the day of preparation) the chief priests and the Pharisees assembled before Pilate and said, "Sir, we remember that while that deceiver was still alive he said, 'After three days I will rise again.' So give orders to secure the tomb until the third day. Otherwise his disciples may come and steal his body and say to the people, 'He has been raised from the dead,' and the last deception will be worse than the first." Pilate said to them, "Take a guard of soldiers. Go and make it as secure as you can." So they went with the soldiers of the guard and made the tomb secure by sealing the stone. **Matthew 27:57-66**

It is the Sabbath.

Last night Joseph of Arimathea asked for and received Jesus' body as they took it down from the cross. He wrapped it with great care and laid it in a tomb, his own new tomb carved into the rock. Joseph got to say his final goodbye, to spend several quiet

232

moments with the crucified Savior, and then he rolled a stone over the mouth of the tomb and left.

Mary and Mary sat hidden by the shadows watching Joseph take care of their King. They watched his every move, but they did not approach him. Instead, they watched him leave and wept as I now do.

There is no way for me to roll away that heavy stone that seals where Jesus now lies. I can't say goodbye like Joseph did. And I want to. I desperately want to. I want to see Him one last time, kiss His cheek like His betrayer did, but kiss His cheek in love, deep, deep love. I want to tell Him I miss Him.

But more than anything, I want Him to come back.

He said He would, didn't He?

In my sadness, I can't remember what He said specifically. But I remember there was something he said about how He was laying down His life - it was His choice. To that, I know He said He has the authority to take it up again. So why doesn't He? Why is He still dead in that tomb?

I stand in the shadows of the Sabbath's early morning light looking around for the others. Where have they gone? Are Mary and Mary still here? What about Peter? Surely he should have deemed it important to come back by now. To admit and acknowledge not only that he knew Jesus but loved Him deeply.

It is so quiet here my breath sounds like the rushing of the winds from yesterday's storm.

I am alone.

Deeply alone.

I am scared and grieving and filled with a raging doubt. I want to go in search of the disciples - Peter, John, Mary, Mary the mother of Jesus, and the others. But I'm afraid to leave. I'm afraid to miss Him because He said He was the Christ. The Messiah.

What if I leave and He comes back to this place?

I hear sandals scraping the gravel and my heart beats faster because maybe, maybe…

But there are too many footsteps. It's not His dusty feet that approach.

Perhaps the disciples are coming. I hope deeply they will join me here on this vigil of waiting and wondering.

From my spot here in the garden growth I squint through the sunlight that burns brightly overhead now to see who will appear. My heart breaks, fills with an overpowering aches as I take in the sight of Roman guards marching toward the tomb as if Jesus is still a threat that must be stopped. There are 16 of them, and they space themselves out surrounding the heavy stone, not far from one another, keeping watch over the tomb and over the garden. The leading priests and Pharisees accompany them, nodding approvingly as the guards apply the Roman seal to the stone and take their positions.

Are Pharisees really still so afraid?

Do they feel no remorse whatsoever?

I sink to the ground, my legs too weak to hold me up any longer. With all the power I can muster in my heart and mind and spirit I will Jesus to push aside the stone and step out like Lazarus.

Where are you? Why have you left us here?

My prayers seem barely to make it close to God's throne; I am too angry and too afraid and too hurt. My grief is as big and heavy as that stone the Roman guard now surrounds.

As the Pharisees turn to leave, I see satisfied smiles on their faces. I want to run at them and hurt them, beating them with my fists and my anguish. But it's not worth it because they are not worth it.

Recalling Jesus' words, I wipe the dust from the bottoms of my feet and turn away, retreating into the shadows where I can see the tomb and keep watch over the guards and maybe find some rest. Though I want to be with the disciples, I *need* to be here, close to my where my Savior is. I need Him.

I need Jesus, but for this moment, I will settle for being near where His body is laid as I watch and wonder, cleave and question, weep and pray.

Prayer

Dear Jesus, I cannot imagine what that first Sabbath day following your crucifixion was like for your disciples. You, crucified before their eyes, their emotions roiling, their fear gnawing in their stomachs and creeping up into their chests. So much was unknown to them that day even though you tried to prepare them and tell them what to expect. Help me, Jesus, to dwell in that first in between, that first Sabbath day after your death, so that I can absorb the full meaning of your death and the sacrifice you made for me. Thank you, Jesus, for dying for me so that I might live. Thank you for taking the punishment that should have been mine. Let me dwell here in quiet reflection today, Lord. Thank you.

Additional Scripture for Reflection

Mark 15:33-47

Luke 23:44-56

John 19:28-42

Easter Sunday: Oh, Glorious Day!

Now very early on the first day of the week, while it was still dark, Mary Magdalene came to the tomb and saw that the stone had been moved away from the entrance. So she went running to Simon Peter and the other disciple whom Jesus loved and told them, "They have taken the Lord from the tomb, and we don't know where they have put him!" Then Peter and the other disciple set out to go to the tomb. The two were running together, but the other disciple ran faster than Peter and reached the tomb first. He bent down and saw the strips of linen cloth lying there, but he did not go in. Then Simon Peter, who had been following him, arrived and went right into the tomb. He saw the strips of linen cloth lying there, and the face cloth, which had been around Jesus' head, not lying with the strips of linen cloth but rolled up in a place by itself. Then the other disciple, who had reached the tomb first, came in, and he saw and believed. (For they did not yet understand the scripture that Jesus must rise from the dead.)

So the disciples went back to their homes. But Mary stood outside the tomb weeping. As she wept, she bent down and looked into the tomb. And she saw two angels in white sitting where Jesus' body had been lying, one at the head and one at the feet. They said to her, "Woman, why are you weeping?" Mary replied, "They have taken my Lord away, and I do not know where they have put him!" When she had said this, she turned around and saw

Jesus standing there, but she did not know that it was Jesus.

Jesus said to her, "Woman, why are you weeping? Who are you looking for?" Because she thought he was the gardener, she said to him, "Sir, if you have carried him away, tell me where you have put him, and I will take him." Jesus said to her, "Mary." She turned and said to him in Aramaic, "Rabboni" (which means Teacher). Jesus replied, "Do not touch me, for I have not yet ascended to my Father. Go to my brothers and tell them, 'I am ascending to my Father and your Father, to my God and your God.'" Mary Magdalene came and informed the disciples, "I have seen the Lord!" And she told them what Jesus had said to her.

On the evening of that day, the first day of the week, the disciples had gathered together and locked the doors of the place because they were afraid of the Jewish leaders. Jesus came and stood among them and said to them, "Peace be with you." When he had said this, he showed them his hands and his side. Then the disciples rejoiced when they saw the Lord. So Jesus said to them again, "Peace be with you. Just as the Father has sent me, I also send you." And after he said this, he breathed on them and said, "Receive the Holy Spirit. If you forgive anyone's sins, they are forgiven; if you retain anyone's sins, they are retained."

Now Thomas (called Didymus), one of the twelve, was not with them when Jesus came. The other disciples told him, "We have seen the Lord!" But he replied, "Unless I see the wounds from the nails in his hands, and

*put my finger into the wounds from the nails, and put my
hand into his side, I will never believe it!"*

*Eight days later the disciples were again together in
the house, and Thomas was with them. Although the doors
were locked, Jesus came and stood among them and said,
"Peace be with you!" Then he said to Thomas, "Put your
finger here, and examine my hands. Extend your hand and
put it into my side. Do not continue in your unbelief, but
believe." Thomas replied to him, "My Lord and my
God!" Jesus said to him, "Have you believed because you
have seen me? Blessed are the people who have not seen
and yet have believed."*

*Now Jesus performed many other miraculous signs
in the presence of the disciples, which are not recorded in
this book. But these are recorded so that you may believe
that Jesus is the Christ, the Son of God, and that by
believing you may have life in his name.* **John 20:1-31**

I wake in the same spot where last night I sat and watched
Joseph of Arimathea lay Jesus' body in the grave, and where I wept
and prayed and wept some more. The sun has not yet risen and the
air has a slight chill, though I wonder if the chill I feel is more
from grief than the morning darkness.

I look across at the grave of my Savior expecting to see the
Roman guard still standing watch over the tomb. And yet...

Is it the darkness? The sleep in my eyes? The longing of my
soul?

The Roman guard is gone and the stone is moved, the mouth of the tomb a gaping wound once more in the face of the rocks. What happened while I dozed? What have the Pharisees done now? Wasn't His pain, His suffering, His death enough for them?

I take shaky breaths and make my way through dew-covered grass and across roughened gravel paths hoping to take a closer look. I want to make sure my eyes aren't playing tricks on me and when I near the heavy stone I see they are not - the stone that yesterday was sealed and guarded by the Roman soldiers indeed has been rolled away. I can feel my heart, each beat pumping anxious uncertainty through me. My hands shake.

I want to examine the tomb, but do I dare? It is eerie quiet and I'm afraid what I will see if I duck my head inside, into the darkness inside.

There is movement closer to the tomb and I stop and watch Mary and the other women as they discover the rolled away stone. Leaving the others behind, Mary runs out of the garden and is swallowed by the morning mist as the sun rises, setting the garden aglow with its red and orange hues.

These women, these strong, fiercely loyal followers of Jesus who have not fled or hidden or betrayed or abandoned, engage in whispered conversations. Though I do not hear their words, I hear their passion for this King they seek to anoint.

Behind me I hear the sound of running feet, pounding along the road to the garden tomb. John and Peter break through the trees draped in the colors of dawn only to stop short at the open mouth of the tomb.

Mary joins the other women and the group embraces, a tangle of arms and hair and tears, hands clutching spices for the

Savior. Tears spill from my eyes and my own breath is ragged as I inch to the entrance of the grave. My eyes rest upon the abandoned burial linens that look as if the body of Jesus simply evaporated, not like someone came and took His body away.

Where are you? I ask the empty darkness, because this isn't how this is supposed to work. *Where have you gone?*

Peter and John leave, offering no words to any of us. The women watch them go but turn their eyes back to the grave. Like they did at the cross, they stay. Mary stays. She mourns and she weeps, and I can see her heart breaking into pieces. Like my own. Broken shards of my heart pierce each breath. The weight of His death made ever greater by His absence - He is gone; the tomb is empty.

But when I look again, it is *not* empty.

Instead there are two men sitting where Jesus was lain by Joseph. I hear them speak, their voices deep and thunder-loud. They don't understand our tears; clearly they know something we do not. My head aches as much as my heart as I sift my thoughts and these circumstances for possible explanations.

Beside me, I sense movement. I see a figure out of the corner of my eye moving toward her. Toward me.

And, then, there He is, standing there. I can barely breathe and I cannot take my eyes take off of Him. I want to throw myself into His arms, but something in His eyes discourages me from doing so. It's a look unfamiliar to me and I tremble.

In the face of my confusion and Mary's grief, His eyes overflow with tenderness and love, His face more familiar now. He speaks her name; He speaks my name. His voice a whisper that brushes each of my senses, and I know. I see Him as He truly is. I see Him in Truth and in Light.

Jesus.

If ever a moment were worthy of a hallelujah, this is it. Jesus stands here, raised from the dead. Two days ago, I saw Him crucified on the cross. Today, He stands beside me talking to me like He did only days ago. As if we are not standing outside the tomb where He was buried.

His eyes lock with mine and joy wracks my soul as much as my sobs did yesterday. "It's really you," I whisper. "You're really here."

"It is, because I AM."

He is everything He said He was and I marvel at it all. I wonder about it all.

Who is this resurrected Jesus? When He shows up in that locked room with the disciples, does He look like the man with whom they traveled for three years? Does He sound the same? Does He look at them the same?

Who is this resurrected Jesus? Surely, He is no longer both man and God. Surely now, He is only God. He is the risen Lord, the resurrected Savior, the one true and eternal Son of God. Soon He will breathe out the Holy Spirit on them and instruct them; He will send them out and meet them back in Galilee.

But I am still wondering at this miracle of God. This miracle that *is* God, that is the man Jesus raised from the dead, who is now raised and walking among those He loves.

There is so much more to learn as the disciples go forth from this place to preach the Good News and I look forward to all there is to learn from those moments. But right now, today, on this first Easter morning, I am content to sit with the disciples and stare up at this risen Jesus. I am content to sit and bask in this amazing miracle. I am content to let the joy that comes from being in His resurrected presence flow over me and through me, to sit dazzled by the sight of Him, to watch Him in wonder and to wonder.

To wonder, who is this God we serve?

To wonder, who is this God who endured all hell and humiliation and death and now is risen?

To wonder, who is this God who loves me like this?

To wonder, who is this God who is so amazing He took my place and He holds in His hands my every breath, my heart, my life.

Just like the grave could not contain Him and death could not defeat Him, words cannot describe Him.

To know Him even a little on this side of heaven requires a heart to which He can speak. A heart that He can fill with His truth and His love *and himself.* Only then can one begin to understand who this God is. Only then can these events come to be more than just a story, but to be life itself. New life. Redeemed life. Resurrected life. Only when we sit at His dusty feet and seek His face do we find His heart.

And like Jesus, I am resurrected today. The death and decay of this world's worries and despair and hopelessness cannot contain me nor defeat me. I live in hope. I live in faith. I live in love. I live in Jesus.

And because of that, I cannot help but shout out, *Hallelujah. He lives. Hallelujah.*

Prayer

Dear Jesus, how amazing it must have been for Mary and for the disciples that day, to see You standing before them. What awe must have overcome them to realize who You were, that indeed You were, You *are* their Lord and their Savior. Lord, I pray that today as I celebrate your Resurrection, as I celebrate on this Easter Sunday, that I will celebrate with the awe and wonder and joy Your original disciples experienced that first Easter Sunday. God, my words cannot convey or capture who You are. Thank You for Your victory that pours over me today and every day because You took my place on the cross and defeated the enemy and the grave.

Additional Scripture for Reflection

1 Corinthians 15:51-58

Romans 8:31-39

Luke 8:1-15